PRESCRIPTIONS FOR A
HEALTHY FAMILY BUSINESS

D. Wayne Rivers

Published by The Family Business Institute, Inc.
3701 National Dr., Ste. 103
Raleigh, North Carolina 27612
(919) 783-1880

www.familybusinessinstitute.com

Although the authors and publishers have made every effort to ensure the accuracy and completeness of information contained in this book, we assume no responsibility for errors, inaccuracies, omissions, or inconsistencies herein. Any perceived slights of people, places, or organizations is unintentional. Readers should use their own judgment and consult reputable advisors for specific applications to their individual problems. None of the comments in this book are to be construed as individual advice.

ISBN 0-9653193-2-6

Table of Contents

Chapter Four

Chapter Five

Chapter Six

Chapter Seven

Chapter Eight

Chapter Nine

Chapter Ten

INTRODUCTION

"The business of America is business."- Calvin Coolidge

If we were to modify President Coolidge's quote, we might say the business of America is *family business*. The family firm is the backbone of the American economy. Researchers Russ Alan Prince and Karen Maru File estimate that there are about 23.3 million non-farm businesses in the United States. Of those, 99% are identified as "small businesses," that is, those with fewer than 500 employees. Small businesses employ 62% of the private work force and are responsible for 64% of the private gross domestic product. New businesses have been growing at about 3% annually in recent years making the United States economy the envy of the world. It goes without saying that the majority of the startup companies which have contributed to our explosive expansion since the 1980's are family and closely held businesses. As the statistics demonstrate, family business is big business.

However, it is difficult to learn about family businesses. When you pick up the morning newspaper or hear a television reporter talk about business, why is it that there is no mention of family business? Why is it that family businesses seem to be a mystery to people - not the least of whom are family business members themselves?

Part of the answer has to do with the fact that it is easy for the media to report on public, Fortune 500 type companies. These companies have public relations staffs filled with media savvy experts who are able to get information about their companies into the public domain as fast as an e-mail or fax.

Family businesses are very different. They spend very little time and energy promoting themselves to anyone other than their direct customers. Furthermore, family businesses are private businesses. If a reporter were to call a family business owner and ask for information on his company like "what were your revenues last year?" he would be apt to get a stony silence, or more likely, a hang-up.

Family businesses dominate the landscape of corporate America in many ways, but very little is known about them. However, in the last ten years there have been a score of books published seeking to dispel myths and provide legitimate information about family businesses.

Our first book, *You Don't Have Die to Win - Success and Succession for Family Businesses*, was among them when it was published in 1996. It sought to shed light on the nature of family businesses, the necessary steps family businesses could and should take to perpetuate themselves, as well as serving as a basic how-to manual which explained many of the arcane and highly technical business succession and planning tools commonly used by lawyers, CPAs, and financial planners.

The target audience for both books remains the same. This work is for people who are parts of families in business, who work in a family business, or who serve family businesses in professions like law, accounting, or counseling. That is not to discount its usefulness to those who have an intellectual curiosity about family businesses, but it is most closely tailored for those who have a direct relationship - blood, professional, or otherwise - with a family enterprise. The purpose of this book is to provide a manual for perpetuating business families.

Family is the most important word in the term family business. While scores of articles, books, and research papers have been written about the fundamentals of business succession and estate planning, comparatively few books have been written about the interpersonal relationships in family enterprises. A family business is a very confusing place to work. If you work in a family business, and the boss expresses anger at a development in your area of responsibility, how are you to respond? Is that person acting in his capacity as your father, your boss, or the majority stockholder of your corporation? How do you feel about disappointing not only your boss but also your father? Working in a family enterprise carries with it not only the normal pros and cons of everyday employment, but also the serious downside potential of damage to parent, child, or sibling relationships. Family business employment often increases opportunity for those who pursue it, but it also increases the downside potential - the emotional risk - and makes a family business livelihood an insecure proposition at times.

This book, then, is designed to help identify the boundaries between family, business operations, and ownership, how you can better understand the other members of your family whether or not you work with them, and how you can communicate more effectively and harmoniously with others who are important to you. It has very little to do with financial issues: there are many other places to find helpful information on wealth preservation, buy-sell agreements, tax strategies, and financial products. *Prescriptions For a Healthy Family Business* is a tool to help with problems which are much more difficult - those that have to do with relationships, constructive communication, and family harmony.

For the sake of writing simplicity, there are many places in this book where we will use the shorthand of he/his or she/hers rather than the more complicated he/she pronouns. This is simply a tool for clearer writing and is not meant to imply that the contributions of women or men are in any way inferior relative to each other. Statistics tell clearly that most of the new, startup enterprises in America are headed by females; in fact, the trend has been growing for some time. We recognize that, are sensitive to it, and don't mean to slight anyone in our reading audience by favoring one gender over the other.

Over the last 10 years, family business planning has grown into a sizable industry comprised generally of academics, CPAs, financial planners, and lawyers. However, in surveying the family business planning done by most professionals, our observation is that legal, technical, and money solutions are generally *wrong* - unless family issues are addressed *first*. Family and interpersonal issues are categorically ignored by most of the professionals who purport to aid family businesses. While professionals do sound work in most occasions, they're not equipped by training, history, or disposition to tackle tough communications and emotional issues. Consequently, most families are left with huge gaps in their long range planning which critically diminish the value and effectiveness of the planning process. Sometimes, even the simplest transition of a tiny business from one generation to the next becomes a terribly complex, emotionally loaded task, and that is where family businesses need the most help.

We hope you enjoy this book. The feedback from our first book was tremendous, and we have been able to integrate many of the comments and experiences shared by other family businesses into this one as well as into our other publications.

If you have questions or comments, you may contact us at:

The Family Business Institute, Inc.
Phone: (919) 783-1880
Email: info@familybusinessinstitute.com
Web: www.familybusinessinstitute.com

Our mission is to provide complete solutions to help family businesses maximize their family and organizational success, and we hope you will find this a helpful tool on your family business journey.

Wayne Rivers

October 29, 2004

CHAPTER ONE

FAMILY BUSINESSES AND THEIR OWNERS

PRESCRIPTION: Create awareness of yourself, your family, and your business. Address the four dynamics of the family enterprise as a whole rather than as individual, unrelated parts.

Family businesses are much more about family than business. The problems and difficulties inherent in managing and owning a family company are more human and relationship oriented than they are technical and money oriented.

Family businesses are families *first*. Family business owners (FBO's) usually start their companies when in their mid-thirties. By that time they have much more life experience as family members, husbands, and fathers than they have as business leaders. Since most FBOs are what Michael Gerber calls "technicians suffering from an entrepreneurial seizure," they have little formal management or business training. When they run into challenges, as they must, they fall back on their biological, emotional experiences on for decision-making instead of their formal business or technical training.

Family businesses begin as families, and each family has its own unique unwritten rules, values, histories, and communication methods. These variables each have impacts on the business in different ways, sometimes positive and sometimes not. Therefore, a family business cannot be truly understood unless there is an understanding of the family and individuals behind the company.

In order to help you understand your family business better, in this chapter we will outline the starkly different natures of the family and the business and the four dimensions of overlap that create strife and conflict in family businesses.

The Family

A study of 60 family businesses by Joyce McLaughlin and Noel Byrne found that the major benefit of a family business was the commitment and dependability of relatives. In another study, 52 of 59 family businesses reported stress and conflict in some aspect of managing the family/business relationship. What are the unique attributes associated with families which add strength and resilience to a family business?

Families are about:

- Love
- Caring
- Unconditional acceptance
- Generational hierarchy
- Emotion
- Informality
- Closeness
- Loyalty
- Commitment
- Stability
- Relationships
- Growth and development
- Safety
- Support
- Tradition

A family is a private world of emotional support and nurturing. Families are constantly changing because the people within them are constantly changing. The changes usually take place gradually and incrementally over long periods of time; however, some changes like death, crippling injury, marital separation, etc. are virtually instantaneous.

Families, like businesses, have definable, traceable life phases that are important factors in how they function. The first phase of family life could be called "The Dreamers." The Dreamers are generally newly wed or have not been married long and are adjusting to married life. They are in their 30's, perhaps just beginning to have children. Once the children have arrived, the Dreamers must learn how to parent. Family business owners generally start their enterprises in the Dreamer stage. In addition to all the other stresses associated with marriage and children, one or both of the spouses is working unbelievably long hours to get the fledgling enterprise off the ground. Often in the Dreamer stage, the spouse who is not working in the family company begins to resent the amount of time and energy the business demands from the other partner.

Generally, the business demands some time from both spouses. They discuss business decisions together, and often spouses help take care of the administrative and bookkeeping chores. In the past, the husband took the leading role in the business, although that arrangement has certainly shifted in the last 10 years.

Young children form their opinions of the family business based on how they see it from their home perspectives. Many children have unconsciously made decisions about whether or not to enter the family enterprise based on the types of dinner table conversations they heard from Mom or Dad. If the tone is one of frustration, aggravation, and constant worry, the children are likely to form negative opinions about the business. If the conversations consist of all success and glory, the children form unrealistic expectations of what business is like. It is important when you carry your business home with you to remember that other people in your house are watching and learning from you constantly. If you have any inkling that at some point in the future you would like other family members to come into your enterprise with you, you must market it intelligently from the beginning. It is impossible to tell a college graduate that the family business is a great place to work if she's heard 22 years of continual frustration over lazy employees, fickle customers, unreliable vendors, and tension between family members.

The second phase of family life is "Letting Go." This phase begins 10 to 15 years after the Dreamers phase. The parents are in mid-life (meaning ages forty to about fifty). Some of the children may be adults now and may have made the decision to enter the family business. Although the business is still on a track of growth, the early phase of struggling for every dollar of revenue and squeezing every expense dollar for savings is in the past, and the business operations have become more stable.

The parents have had to learn to let go of their children to go off to college, develop serious romantic relationships, get married, choose their livelihoods, etc. The family business owner or the "copreneur" couple has had to let go of some of the business operations to avoid throttling business growth. They now have a staff of competent people who can take care of many basic day-to-day functions.

Couples in the Letting Go phase must also begin to take care of their aging parents. Their first brush with mortality comes when the aging parents begin to grow ill and die. The Letting Go comes from both directions; children are leaving the nest, and elderly parents are slowing down and/or passing away.

The third phase for families is the "Testing" phase. This phase comes 10 to 15 years later still. Now the parents are about 55 to 65 years old. Their children range in age from late teens to perhaps early 30s. Relationships are more complex in the Testing phase. Now, for the first time, in-laws are introduced to the nuclear family. Children are grown, have children of their own, and have their own ideas about how to do things. Some of the children have likely entered the family company while others have not. In fact, a survey conducted by The Family Business Institute in 1996 indicated that approximately 80% of family companies have children in the business while another 80% have children not employed in the business. The responses indicate that the typical business family has at least one child working in the company and at least one child who does not work in the company creating potential sibling rivalry issues of fairness and favoritism.

The tests in this stage of family life are numerous. Can everyone in this business family work together productively and harmoniously? Can the business grow large enough to support the income needs and dreams of multiple family members? Can all the family members who choose to earn their way into the family company find a meaningful career path? How is the business viewed among different family members? There is a great deal of pride in most family business companies. The business stands for something and has provided jobs, goods, and services for many people in the community. The business may be the main reason for the affluence and influence of the entrepreneurial family. There are some question marks, however, about the successful business. Most family members want to know why there is never any cash if the business is doing so well. Why are things so tight? Most business families live very modest lifestyles through the Testing phase. Most, if not all, of the profits are plowed back into the business to fuel growth. The spouse of the entrepreneur may wonder when they will have an opportunity to slow down and enjoy life more. The children of the entrepreneur begin to worry about this highly focused, highly motivated personality and whether or not he has set himself up for a heart attack or other life threatening illness. Everyone wants to know why this mission is still so compelling when life should be getting a bit smoother. Good communication and productive interpersonal relationships are essential in the Testing phase of family development.

The fourth stage of family development is the "Transition" stage. This phase involves sharing and/or passing leadership in the family and the business. Mom and Dad are in their 60s to age 80 and the children are in their 30s to 50s. Families in the Transition stage are trying to achieve a delicate balance. The senior generation may be interested in "passing the baton," but they may have 20 to 30 more years of life ahead. The head of the business is finding it desperately hard to separate himself from the company to which he devoted his life for 40 years. He is talking about leaving the scene of his greatest glories and leaving behind a significant part of his adult identity. Financial security for Mom and Dad becomes a critical issue; everyone has to look at the family business to determine how many hogs can feed from one trough. Mom and Dad are not about to let go if it means losing their old age financial security. The Transition phase is one of the biggest times for conflict, argument, and anxiety in the family or the family firm.

In most family companies, there is no formal management or ownership succession plan for the business. A recent study by the Associated General Contractors of America determined that 58% of their members admitted to having no formal succession plans (and empirical evidence suggests the figure is much higher). A vital job for the head of the family business is to prepare for a smooth passing of the baton to the next generation. Passing the baton is a topic for more discussion in a later chapter.

Families, irrespective of their stage of development, lend a special strength to business as the company draws on the values, traditions, and selflessness of the owner family. However, when the family is struggling, anger, tension, confusion, and the strangled communication of family members can be disastrous for the family business.

The Business

Businesses require different characteristics than families for success. Businesses are:

- Task based
- Impersonal
- Conditional
- Short lived
- Cold, emotionally detached
- Require formality, policies, and procedures
- Demand accountability
- Results oriented
- Profit centered
- Unstable
- Neutral with respect to relationships
- Performance driven
- Seek change

A business is a visible world for action and reaction and is measured by the amount of profit it produces. Businesses do not play favorites; the awards go to those who can build better mousetraps to stay ahead of the competition.

While families are in constant stages of gradual change, businesses tend to change in fits and starts. There are plateaus of little change followed by explosive growth to the next level. The life span of a business can be traced in four phases: Wonder, Thunder, Plunder and Blunder.

In the "Wonder" stage, the entrepreneur strikes out on her own with little more than faith in herself that she can birth a successful business. Generally she scrapes together as much capital as she can get, but it's never enough. She has learned a skill, developed a process, or found a way to provide a good or service that she considers to be superior to others on the market. Armed with this knowledge and little else, she strikes out. She doesn't know anything about running a business; that will undoubtedly come to her as she needs it. In the Wonder stage, she's never sure if there is truly a market for what she does. Day-to-day survival is a struggle, and work days are 12 hours or longer. The quest to create a successful business consumes the entrepreneur.

In the second stage, "Thunder", life becomes a little easier. The entrepreneur has come to the realization that there is a market for what she provides. She's making a name for herself, and, while the tasks are still difficult, she can see the light at the end of the tunnel. She still works hard, but now there are other employees to share the load. No longer must she get the mail, make the deposits, take the orders, provide the goods, and do everything else. There are rudimentary procedures and systems to handle routine tasks. Cash flow, while still precious, is a little less tenuous. No longer does the entrepreneur have to place her paycheck in the center desk drawer until there are funds enough to cover it. The business is creating Thunder in the marketplace.

In the "Plunder" stage, the business is maturing and has created a serious market niche for itself. People and systems are humming along, and the business has become a cash cow for the entrepreneur. Life is good, and the rewards are flowing from the pump priming which took place in stages one and two. While the Plunder stage has its rewards, the entrepreneur is having a much harder time keeping control of the disparate parts of her organization. There are expanding opportunities, but she also feels the greatly increased stress that comes from growth.

The final stage of business life is the "Blunder" stage. In the Blunder stage, the company's growth surpasses the ability of the entrepreneur to lead it. It is rare to find a person who starts a business and retains the perspective to admit that she doesn't have the skills necessary to provide the professional management needed to take the enterprise to the next level. What usually happens is that the entrepreneur tries to continue to grow but without the structure and business expertise needed to manage effectively. It doesn't take long before the senior managers in the organization realize that the hands on, controlling style upon which the company was founded and built is unworkable for the future. However, no one can confront the entrepreneur for fear that "the messenger will be shot." Family members and top senior managers either stagnate or move on to other companies where they can follow a professional leadership track. The failure to professionalize and systematize is the colossal blunder that most entrepreneurs make which ultimately determines that their companies will either stagnate, shrink, or fail.

A second Blunder is in management and ownership succession. Most entrepreneurs state that they fervently desire a continued life for their businesses after they are gone. However, most entrepreneurs never plan for that to take place. In a classic study of why family firms fail, the University of Connecticut determined that the second most common reason for failure of a family company is the lack of a formal succession plan. Because of her track record of success, the founder believes she is Wonder Woman - nothing can ever happen to her. She says things like, "if I die..."

Professor James Lea, of the University of North Carolina, in his book *Keeping It In The Family*, documents a study which demonstrates that successful transitions of family companies are closely connected to the length of time spent planning for those transitions. Without a well conceived and executed succession plan, the business cannot continue while maximizing its potential.

In either of the Blunder scenarios, what was once a cash cow becomes a rotting carcass. It's truly sad to see once proud and successful businesses humbled because of predictable and avoidable mistakes made by entrepreneurial families. Lifetimes of hard work and pride are decimated. Lives are affected. Fortunes vanish. None of this has to happen. It is never too early to anticipate the steps necessary for

9

continued prosperity and growth across the generations. Avoiding the subject will not make it go away, nor will it cure the condition. Only when the owners, senior management, and family stakeholders address business continuation issues can workable solutions be found which will eliminate the costly Blunder stage. Family businesses can be rejuvenated; they can be renewed and reinvigorated so that the Wonder and Thunder stages are repeated for a new era of family business success.

There is relatively little in common between the natures of a typical family and a typical business organization, and the stark incompatibilities make it clear why family businesses present so many challenges.

The Four Distinct Family Business Dynamics

In any business family system, there are four distinct family business dynamics at play.

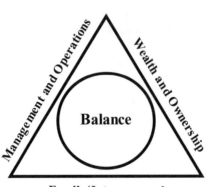

Family/Interpersonal

In the model above, the base of the family business triangle is the business family system, interpersonal relations between family members, and interpersonal relations between members of the business family team. While many people think of businesses as machines that crank out products or services, the truth is that they are populated not by machines but by people. Those people must communicate, lead, follow, be motivated, and handle victory, defeat, and daily challenges effectively. Dealing with the "soft" and human issues and family and interpersonal relations are usually the most delicate and most overlooked areas of need in closely held businesses.

The second side of the family business triangle is the day-to-day management and operations of the enterprise. Management and operations consist of the chain of authority, well defined roles and responsibilities, the administrative functions of the business, delivery of business products and services, marketing and sales, customer service, information technologies, etc.

The third side of the family business triangle is the wealth and ownership dimension. This closely held business dynamic deals with money and power. In founding generations, the owner and manager were generally the same person. However, in subsequent generations, management may consist of one group of people while ownership consists of a different group. Just as managers must have defined roles and responsibilities in the family enterprise, owners do also, but because closely held enterprises generally fail to make a clear distinction between ownership responsibilities and management responsibilities, conflict and confusion result.

Family businesses are also troubled by uncertainty over their estate and wealth distribution planning. While most financial services professionals are perfectly capable of developing estate and tax avoidance strategies, the strategies are usually not in concert with the business family's long term goals and wishes. Effective estate plans must take into account family members' needs for security, relative fairness between employee and non-employee shareholders, and the potentially damaging effects of wealth of the individuals in the group over time.

The fourth dynamic of the family business triangle is BALANCE. Because the family enterprise has such a strong gravitational pull for the families who populate it, people often find their lives out of balance. The business or customers demand 80 hour work weeks, and family communication, health, spirituality, and other areas suffer. In fact, it's the rule rather than the exception that at some point in the life span of the family company, the business drains the life out of the family rather than adding to and enhancing the quality of their lives.

Since all family business systems are composed of the four distinct dynamics above and are all part of a unified family business system, it doesn't make practical sense to attempt to provide solutions on the wealth and ownership side, for example, without simultaneously addressing the intended or unintended effects on the management and operations and family/interpersonal sides. In other words, if a business family hired a management consultant to help streamline operations, there could be unintended consequences from that project which negatively affect the other three dimensions of the family enterprise. A management consultant may recommend that a family member be promoted to a new position of authority and responsibility; however, this may not be consistent with the family's unwritten code that states that same generation siblings should be roughly equal in their power and influence in the company and should be compensated the same. While the management consultant has made a seemingly routine recommendation, he may have unwittingly blundered by asking the business family to make a change that is inconsistent with their family business tradition. It's often unwise and ineffective to attempt to remedy problems in one of the family business dynamics without addressing the "big picture" environment and the other dimensions.

Ownership Evolution of Family Businesses

There are three distinct ownership stages of family enterprises. They are the Founding Owner stage, the Sibling Partner stage, and the Cousin Consortium. Researchers Gersick, Davis, Hampton, and Lansberg in their outstanding book *Generation To Generation* estimate that 75% of all family businesses are owned by one person or by a married couple in the Founding Owner stage. If there are other owners, they are generally holders of only token shares, and they are usually family members who received their corporate stock via gifts. There is usually a "paper" board of directors that is dominated by the founding entrepreneur. The other directors are usually family members who (if they're involved at all) rubber-stamp management's decisions. In fact, in most family companies, the paper board never even meets. Someone on the corporate staff or the corporate attorney is charged with producing minutes from board meetings which exist informally at best.

The capitalization for the start of the company generally comes from the founder, the spouse, or other family members; often the initial startup capital came with emotional strings attached. Companies in the Founding Owner stage often succeed or fail on the vision, energy, competence, and desire of one person. That one person works 50 to 80 hours per week and is a dominating force within the family, not to mention the business. A successful Founding Owner stage company can be the source of both affluence and influence for the founders. The founding owner is able (as sole owner and manager) to choose the next leadership and ownership of the company. In most cases, however, he simply doesn't do it; it happens by default.

The second stage of family business ownership is that of Sibling Partners. Gersick, Davis, Hampton and Lansberg estimate this represents about 20% of the family owned companies in America. Sibling Partnerships are owned by two or more brothers, sisters, or other sibling combinations. They may or may not be active in the business. If active employee and non-active, non-employee shareholders exist, they have different interests in the future of the business. The active shareholders are usually interested in growing the business and their equity interests. The passive shareholders are generally interested in current income returns and are less interested in growth for future generations. In Sibling Partnerships, the need to compensate non-employee family members without robbing the business of capital needed for growth becomes an important issue. Another critical issue is who is in voting control of the business. The Sibling Partner form of ownership is difficult to sustain over time because of the inherent conflict between employee and non-employee siblings.

The third stage of family business ownership is the Cousin Consortium. This represents approximately 5% of the family companies in America. There are generally three generations or more of ownership. There is a broad range of ages, family relationships, places of residence, marital status, and wealth among the varying owners. It is not uncommon for 10 or more shareholders to have stock in the company. Generally, no single branch of the family has enough voting power to control the vote on important issues. There is a mixture of employee family members and non-employee family members. Family bonds are difficult to maintain; for the first time many of the shareholders of the corporation never really knew the founding entrepreneur.

A key challenge for Cousin Consortiums is managing the complexity of the shareholder group. Family conflicts that may have occurred one or two generations ago are often amplified and transmitted via family myths and fables. Many family members have very little in common *except* their ownership interests in the company.

Another key challenge for Cousin Consortiums is creating a market for the stock - what is management to do when a non-employee family member wants to sell out? From where does the capital come? It is essential to create rules for ownership of the business stock, employment in the family company, and sales of family business stock *before* they become necessary. After disagreement or conflict has broken out, it is too late to establish amicable, fair rules for everyone in the ownership group. A common step for multi-generation corporations to take is to consider going public if business conditions warrant. Another common outcome for Cousin Consortiums is that one or more strong third or fourth generations leaders emerge who is able to create the vision and capital necessary to buy back shares and return the company to a Founding Owner or Sibling Partnership stage.

A third key challenge is driving the business forward. Since no controlling interest exists in the company, there is often little incentive for risk taking, and the company stagnates for lack of a clear vision.

Transition - A Process, Not an Event!

As if family businesses weren't complicated enough, there is a yet another consideration which adds an additional measure of complexity; it is transition. Time renders even the greatest family business leader incapable of handling the mental and physical demands of the company. The march of time makes transition inevitable no matter how much it is avoided, feared, postponed, or fought.

Normally people think of transition as an event. They associate it with death, retirement, etc. That is not the case. Succession is not one thing; it is many things. In its best form, transition is a process that occurs over time in a planned, orderly progression. Handing the torch to a new leader cannot be done overnight. The best analogy for describing the process of transition is the analogy of a runner in a relay race. When the first runner is finishing his leg, the second runner in the sequence takes off and builds up his speed to exactly match that of the first runner. The reason they match speeds is to create a smooth and uneventful handoff of the baton. Think for a minute what the result would be if the runner of the second leg stood still at his start line awaiting the handoff from the first runner; it would be a catastrophic collision! This is often exactly what family businesses do. The second runner, the leader of the second generation for example, stands still waiting for direction from the runner of the first leg, the founding entrepreneur. If the founding entrepreneur does not do his part to prepare the leader of the second generation, difficulties abound, and the transition is considerably less than smooth.

Why is transition such an important time for a family company? Some family business commentators estimate that as many as 85% of the crises faced by family companies arise around the issues of transition. Succession isn't simply a financial decision, a management decision, or a family decision but a process that must take place over many years involving leadership development of the successor generation, finding a challenging role for the departing leader, effective business planning, effective financial planning, attention to legal and accounting issues, and accountability on the part of all members of the family. It is a delicate balancing act, and family businesses fail to take it seriously in many instances.

Conclusion

Dealing with family businesses is like juggling. To be a good juggler, you have to keep multiple balls in the air at the same time. In a family business juggling act, it is impossible to deal with only one aspect of the family or the business and still have successful outcomes in the other aspects. Issues that arise have to be dealt with carefully and uniquely depending on the business life cycle and ownership stage positions. It is important to recognize the flashpoints associated with transition so no family members feel their interests aren't given a fair forum. Finally, it is important to treat the whole family business system as the "patient" to achieve the type of balance necessary for the family business to move forward from stability to success to significance.

CHAPTER TWO

UNDERSTANDING FAMILY BUSINESS OWNERS - HEROIC STATURE AND THE HEROIC MISSION

PRESCRIPTION: Recognize that successful family business owners are pursuing the two dreams that all heroes (from ancient mythology to the present) pursue - the dreams of heroic mission and heroic stature. Ultimately, both are illusory.

In a country where business leaders have often been lionized in their communities and in the press, many family business owners come to view themselves as heroes; each sees himself as "the man on the white horse," to use a phrase popularized by Earl Nightingale. They grow to see themselves as heroes who provide jobs, goods and services, opportunities, and affluent lifestyles for their families - and they're correct in their estimations. In a society where so many things are wrong, their entrepreneurial accomplishments stand out like beacons as achievements that are right and good. At some point, however, the concept of businessman as hero with powers far beyond those of mortal men can become damaging to the business and the family. Even heroic family business owners must come to grips with aging, the loss of energy, the loss of mental and physical prowess, and ultimately death.

Family business owners are mortal, and they must come to grips with the fact that their heroic self concepts can get in the way - and even doom their companies to extinction - if they don't take measures to see their dreams continue. This chapter looks at the two elements of heroic self-concept: heroic stature and the heroic mission. It will help the reader understand FBO's as entrepreneurial types, the effect of the heroic image on the children of FBOs, and, finally, moving beyond the reign of the heroic family business leader to a healthy, prosperous future.

Portrait of the Entrepreneurial Type

According to Dr. Daniel Levinson, a man's work is the primary influence of his persona in his adult years. In America, since we have no royalty, we have had to invent it: Movie stars, athletes, and sometimes even politicians are our substitutes for royalty. Not far behind come the leaders of successful family business enterprises. FBO's often become larger-than-life figures in their communities or industries.

To paraphrase Jeffrey Sonnenfeld in *The Hero's Farewell*, what business heroes have in common with the heroes of myth and religion is they not only symbolize dreams and aspirations to their firms and to society in general, but they also are accomplishers of pragmatic goals.

Society admires inspirational leaders who can translate hazy visions into concrete realities. The entrepreneur's sense of purpose and self-worth become linked to the success and well being of the business he spawned. The vision becomes the mission becomes the man.

Dr. Thomas Stanley has done more work on the people who own wealth than any other researcher. He has developed a detailed profile of wealthy individuals as well as of the "average Joe" who works his whole life for someone else. Stanley has reached some startling conclusions. The most surprising is the fact that 80% of America's millionaires are first generation millionaires (in spite of what the media portrays). Over 80% of those first generation millionaires are people who own and operate their own businesses - in short, small business owners. When Dr. Stanley writes and speaks about millionaires, he is referencing directly the vast majority of today's successful family business owners.

Dr. Stanley's research indicates that nearly half of the wealth in America is owned by three and a half percent of households. The average household in America has a net worth of less than $15,000 excluding their home equity. If one discounts the equity in motor vehicles, furniture and other personal property, the typical American household usually has zero financial assets (like stocks and bonds).

Even the top 20% of income earners are not really wealthy. While more than seven million American households have annual incomes over $100,000 per year, their median household net worth is less than $150,000. Excluding home equity, the median net worth for the top quintile falls to less than $60,000. With respect to senior citizens, if you take away social security benefits, about half of Americans over 65 would live in poverty.

In trying to determine what factors contribute to success (and ultimately wealth), Dr. Stanley has discovered seven common denominators. Generally speaking, the wealthy individual is a businessman who has lived in the same town for all of his adult life. He has had only one marriage and remains married. He is generally a compulsive saver and investor. He has made his money his own way by doing his own thing.

He neither had a template for getting rich nor did he receive a large inheritance.

Stanley's seven common denominators of how family business owners accumulate their wealth are as follows:

1. They live well below their means.
2. They allocate time, energy, and money efficiently in ways conducive to building wealth.
3. They believe that financial independence is more important than displaying high social status.
4. Their parents did not provide "economic outpatient" care.
5. Their adult children are economically self sufficient.
6. They are proficient in targeting market opportunities.
7. They choose the right occupation.

Source: The Millionaire Next Door by Thomas J. Stanley, Ph.D.

There are many characteristics that have been documented that are consistent with entrepreneurial activity. Among them are: a high desire for control, inability to adapt to working for someone else, early family experience, etc. But two specific motivations are particularly important. The first is the longing to be an owner/manager instead of an employee who works for someone else; entrepreneurs desire control. It has been said that the greatest fear of the entrepreneur is failure. The second greatest fear of the entrepreneur is success. Often the seeds of failure are sown in the entrepreneur's initial success; for example, the high degree of control he initially exerts over his enterprise and his stubbornness of purpose can become institutionalized into the business. Ultimately the business becomes one that is resistant to structure and hierarchy and resists formalization and sound business practices.

The second key entrepreneurial motivation is the clear vision of a market opportunity and the strong desire to fill that market opportunity with a product or service. FBOs are unusually sophisticated in targeting appropriate market opportunities and have the dogged persistence to see their dreams to fruition.

Entrepreneurs are usually self-financed. A survey by Coopers and Lybrand in 1994 concluded that 73% of entrepreneurs found their start-up capital through personal savings and/or loans from other family members. Only 27% sought outside investors or bank loans. Having family capital (including low cost labor) and the family's willingness to take risks and sacrifice personal security in the early years of the company are two of the most important financial resources available to entrepreneurs.

While the vast majority of the American population can never see themselves taking the risks and making the sacrifices necessary to run their own companies, most entrepreneurs feel that self employment is *less risky* than working for other people. It's ironic to hear family business owners - who are engaged in some of the riskiest fields of business imaginable - talk about how they keep all of their profits in certificates of deposit at their local banks because they believe that investing in the stock market is "too risky!" Entrepreneurs look at risk differently than most people, however. To them, risk is having only one source of income. Most family business owners arrange their affairs so that they have multiple sources of income. Their goal is to create independence, or at least an absence of dependence on others.

Entrepreneurs have a set of core beliefs that cause them to con-clude that they are not engaged in risky businesses. First, they adore the idea of being in control of their destinies. Second, they have confidence that they can solve any problem that confronts them. Third, they are impatient, and, therefore, reluctant to wait to reach the top of a public corporation in the traditional way. They want to be the CEO immediately so they can fulfill their visions; the best way to do that is to own the company. Fourth, they don't want to be limited in income relative to another group of managers who may not work as hard or be as productive. Fifth, they have great courage and are not daunted by facing risk and adversity. Entrepreneurial FBOs have personal resilience, they don't accept the authority of others easily, they rarely, if ever, truly retire, and their business pursuits keep them energized and feeling young in spite of their advancing ages. Other characteristics are the refusal to follow anyone else's model on how to begin and run their companies and a strict reliance on their own judgment and imagination to develop their businesses.

Generally, family owned and operated businesses are places of constant turmoil. Many family business owners talk about the necessity of having to constantly put out fires in their organizations. Interestingly, they thrive on just that activity. They are masters at creating order out of chaos. In fact, when things get too quiet, family business owners and entrepreneurs often "stir the pot" and search for new challenges.

Entrepreneurs are characterized by a strong internal compulsion to create something. They have personal motivation for great achievement. They are unlikely to plan for retirement and acknowledge their advancing ages. They enjoy their work and can't see a time when they will not enjoy coming into the office and getting things done. Even after "retirement," they continue to work in one capacity or another.

Drawing on Dr. Stanley's work, it's possible to narrow down the broad qualities of entrepreneurs and develop a specific portrait of the successful business owning entrepreneur. The prototypical American millionaire looks like the following:

- 57 years old
- Married with three children
- Self employed entrepreneur
- Low tech business
- Spouse does not work outside home
- Average income of $247,000
- Median income of $131,000
- Average household net worth of $3.7 million
- Median household net worth of $1.6 million
- Total annual income less than 7% of net worth
- Average value of home is $320,000
- First generation affluent

- Lives frugally and well below the levels possible
- Meticulous budgeter
- Has a sizable stash of cash as a "rainy day fund"
- College educated (80%)
- Believes in education for children and grandchildren
- Works about 50 hours per week
- Compulsive saver with the vast majority of individual and company profits being plowed back into the business
- Most trusted financial advisor is the certified public accountant
- Is a tightwad
- Most common make of car: Ford
- Most common model of car: Jeep Grand Cherokee (about 58% of family business owners drive American cars)
- Highest price paid for suit of clothes $399
- Highest price paid for pair of shoes $140
- Highest price paid for wristwatch $235

Interestingly, the statistics for first generation wealth are fairly constant over time. A survey in the *American Economy* in 1892 concluded that 84% of American millionaires were "*nouveau riche*," having reached the top without the benefit of inherited wealth. In other words, they were self made millionaires.

What do family business owners spend their money on? They're tightwads when it comes to most retail products, but Dr. Stanley found that they do not have price sensitivity when purchasing the following:

- Investment advice and services
- Accounting services
- Tax advice
- Legal services
- Medical care
- Dental care
- Educational opportunities

- Homes and resort homes
- Vacations with their children and grandchildren

One of the most startling findings of Dr. Stanley's work is that "financially independent people are happier than those in their same income/age cohort who are not financially secure." While it is true that money cannot buy happiness, it is a fact that one can never enjoy true happiness if one is always worried where the next meal or rent check will come from. Having accumulated significant financial and business assets over time, the successful family business owner is free to flower as a human being without the day to day survival struggles that have plagued mankind for most of human history.

Heroic Mission

Family business owners are consumed by their visions or their ideas of what their enterprises could and should be. The vision, although rarely written and infrequently articulated to those around them, is a deep and abiding passion that resembles obsession or love. The vision, as we'll see later, can cause the FBO to be oblivious to things around him, even critically important things like his family, health, and spirituality.

The dream or idea is more than a vague fantasy, yet somewhat less clear than a carefully defined plan. It generates excitement and enthusiasm in the FBO, and, at certain times, it is the most compelling thing in his life. According to psychologist Otto Rank, the vision or heroic drive is an expression of one's effort to survive his own death and to achieve a measure of immortality by leaving a lasting imprint or legacy on society. Often the FBO's identity becomes so intertwined with the identity of the business that anything that affects the enterprise affects him.

The business is the scene of the FBO's greatest triumphs and successes. It is a place where his power and status are confirmed and reconfirmed every day. It is where he is king, master, and benevolent dictator over his realm, and the FBO can get addicted to the sense of his own greatness.

Heroic mission is defined as the drive to make an immortal contribution. Heroic stature, which we will examine more closely in the next section, is defined as the aspect of the FBO's self concept that intertwines his personal identity with his occupational role as business leader.

According to Jeffrey Sonnenfeld's research, a sense of heroic mission stems from the need for strong leaders to justify themselves as the objects of primary value in the universe. What the heroic mission means for the business and the family is that the FBO, in his frenetic race to make his dream come true, may fail to communicate effectively with the people around him. The vision is so clear to him that he can't understand why everyone doesn't see it. He may feel that to do a job right he has to do it himself. He may lose a clear sense of himself as an individual apart from the business. He resents and shuns those who question him or his mission, and becomes defensive and prickly when interrogated. The narrow, laser like focus he brings to the heroic mission can be an impediment as his business grows and the need to professionalize his operation increases. It can also cause serious problems in the family due to his long hours, inability to think about anything that is not business related, lack of time for balance in his life, and impatience with the niceties of providing a loving and nurturing family environment. The vision is a magnificent obsession that crowds out virtually everything else in the family business owner's life. The FBO caught in the creation of a heroic mission is involved in an oppressive, daily struggle to achieve more and more in less and less time. FBOs often compare themselves to other business leaders they read or hear about but don't know personally. They're nontraditional and innovative in developing their heroic missions and businesses. They reinvent the wheel constantly and resist using the models of others in pursuing their ideals. They may like structure, timeliness, and clear guidelines for others, but they like to stay flexible and freewheeling in their own schedules and work habits.

Sonnenfeld's work indicates that family business owners shape their corporate cultures in seven ways:

1. What they pay attention to through measurement and control.
2. How they react to specific incidents and crises.
3. Their recruitment, selection, promotion, and dismissal policies.
4. The authority structures and flows of information they establish.
5. The design of the physical space they administer.
6. Their creation or circulation of stories, legends, or myths that convey the firm's core values.
7. Their formal statements of company philosophy.

Ironically, their strong personalities can lead to corporate cultures which reflect their bad as well good qualities. For example, if an FBO has a dysfunction in his personality such as paranoia, depression, etc., that trait can become a part of the company's collective behavior.

What does the heroic mission mean to the business family? Most significantly, family reactions to strong entrepreneurs tend to be emotional rather than business based. Emotional reactions to entrepreneurs immersed in heroic missions bleed over into family decision-making, and it's impossible to tell where the family business owner stops and the business begins. Children who have a largely absent parent sometimes don't have the opportunities to develop solid skills in dealing with authority figures later in life. They lack effective role models to turn to for advice as they grow up and take on new responsibilities. They don't effectively develop skills of expressing their emotions because they are taught to suppress emotions in an effort to push courageously forward in life. A family business owner caught in a heroic mission can create problems for normal development, especially during the critical teenage years when children must begin the process of creating their individual identities separate and distinct from those of the parents.

Heroic Stature

Heroic stature is the special distinction of position and command that allows a person to stand above the group and thus occupy a unique role in it. As Ralph Waldo Emerson said, "an institution is the length and shadow of one man."

Family business owners are different from other people; their work defines their personal identities. Their actions have a large impact on others including family members, employees, customers, vendors, and many other people whose lives they touch either directly or indirectly. Family business owners are a type of American royalty or folk hero:

- They can serve as symbols of triumphs of individual spirit and vision while tumult rules in other sectors of society.

- They serve as corporate focal points for a collective strategy and group loyalty much like a highly successful sports coach.

- Family business owners so commingle their personal identities with their corporate visions that they lose the personal identity altogether. They define themselves as what they do rather than who they are.

In short, family business owners are cult heroes.

A family business owner with a sense of heroic stature does not accept the limitations generally imposed on lesser people. He rejects traditional barriers to his accomplishments. He can't envision a day when he won't be able to work and lead his company to even higher goals. He refuses to admit that there is a finite period beyond which he is no longer a help but a detriment to the continued success of his enterprise. For family business owners, *retirement equals death*. Psychoanalyst Ernest Becker went so far as to write a book called *Denial of Death* in which he said that a leader "must stand out, be a hero, make the biggest possible contribution toward life, and show that he counts more than anyone or anything else." The FBO's belief in his own uniqueness allows him to bury his intellectual knowledge of his own mortality. It allows him to believe that he can actually avoid death; his vision for his company becomes a plan to ensure his own individual immortality. Family business owners resist retirement and planning for succession simply because they are not finished shaping their heroic endeavors. They always want to come back one more day because they think there is one more chance to build upon their legacies.

Often family business owners build themselves traps. The heavy responsibility of always being the leader means high expectations among others. The heroic self-concept so overwhelms the leader's non-heroic, personal self-concept that he could lose touch with a part of himself forever. In addition to the psychological trap, family business owners often build financial traps. They invest and reinvest so single-mindedly in their companies that they wake up at age 70 and find that 80% or more of their net worth is tied up in their closely held enterprise, and they have no concept of how to effectively draw that equity out over their remaining lifetimes without crippling the business operations and killing their business spawn. While there is a sense of nobility in the development of a successful family enterprise, there are hidden traps as well.

What does the fact that the FBO has developed heroic stature mean to the business family? Simply put, the successful entrepreneur is an awfully hard act to follow. Children of successful entrepreneurs are always aware of the presence of the business which was, in effect, a rival for Dad's attention. For many family business children, the experience of growing up was dominated by the realization that the business was *number one*. Entrepreneurs have a hard time listening to anyone, especially their children. It can be very difficult for children in family business households to constantly seek out Dad's approval and blessing only to find that he is so occupied with business issues that he barely hears what the child is saying. In *Working With The Ones You Love*, Dr. Dennis Jaffe flatly states that a family business is not a good place in which to grow up. Everyone wants to become a hero, but to actually develop into a hero, one must leave home. Jaffe says that "the hero's journey begins when he wakes up to a call, leaves his family, and begins a quest for something important." This quest develops his inner talents. He isn't given a whole self; through the quest, he builds himself. Unfortunately, the family business sometimes does a strange job of short circuiting personal development by making a seductive offer to the hero to stay at home and not grow. The family business is simultaneously a blessing and a trap.

Beyond Heroic Mission and Heroic Stature

Some men make the pursuit of their business vision the central element in their lives and build everything else around it. However, this is illusory. Dr. Levinson describes the central illusion as follows: "if I attain the dream - if I become a great novelist or scientist, if I make a special contribution to humanity or to my clan, if I gain great power - then life will be good and everything really important will come to me." The dream then becomes reaching a specific goal. Unfortunately, most family business owners don't see that a goal is a successive progression; they see only the end. If the family business owner fails to attain that goal, his life will have been a total failure and will have had no value. The illusion is that there is no success short of ultimate success.

Another illusion is that, if the hero is successful in achieving his quest, he will live happily ever after. Discovering that this is not so and dealing with the consequences is a difficult process for highly successful men in their mid-life transitions. Most of the men whose lives are based on the quest for the heroic mission must ultimately deal with the consequences of flawed success if not outright failure.

The wife of the family business owner is often a major victim and beneficiary of his quest. He loves and rewards his wife as long as she performs well in her appointed role. But he can have difficulty regarding her as a whole person and considering her independent gifts and talents.

Eliminating these illusions of heroic mission and heroic stature and reducing the tyranny of the entrepreneurial dream is a major task for men in mid-life transition. Family business owners must work to reduce the excessive power of their dreams to make success less essential and failure less disastrous. They must slowly and painfully pull back from the work that has defined them and try to find balance in other areas of their lives. The maturing family business owner has earned self confidence and pride in his accomplishments. He would like to take it a little easier and begin to harvest some of the profits from his lifetime of work. His success has caused him to make the mistake of thinking that his experience of the past is the only experience he will need to be successful in the future. With the pace of change in our society accelerating, doing things "because that's the way we've always done it here" simply won't work anymore.

Control, that most dear and precious item in the eyes of many family business entrepreneurs, is also an illusion which must be put away. Holding everything close to the vest - whether business or personal - is a recipe for disaster for other members of the family who simply must know what the future looks like for them.

The way a family business owner leaves his company is one of the most important aspects of his legacy. If he leaves willingly, with a written succession plan and with a strong management team in place, his vision can endure for generations to come. If his ultimate departure from the company is characterized by bitterness, rancor, and acrimony, ill feelings may endure which will affect every personal and professional relationship he has developed over time.

It takes a certain set of skills to create and nurture a business from the ground up. It takes a very different set of skills to manage a mature business after sales have reached $20 to $100 million or beyond.

Conclusion

The senses of heroic mission and heroic stature reflect the deep needs of the family business owner to create a legacy which lives beyond his lifetime to ensure a measure of immortality. However, heroic concept, if not tempered by common sense and real maturity, can cripple the ability of the family enterprise to succeed beyond the first generation.

Bill Rosenberg, the founder of Dunkin' Donuts, had a wonderful perspective: "What have you accomplished if what you have created dies when you do? The only true accomplishment is having created and organized something so that it will succeed and grow after you are gone." Recognizing the illusory nature of the dreams of heroic mission and heroic stature and acting wisely to perpetuate the family business will allow an FBO to create a legacy which can be an enduring monument to his vision and greatness.

CHAPTER THREE

UNDERSTANDING FAMILY BUSINESS OWNERS -
THE MALE AGING PROCESS

PRESCRIPTION: Recognize and understand that there are evolutionary forces beyond your control that are partially driving the way you think and feel. Learn how those forces affect your business and family lives.

Social scientists have conducted innumerable studies on the development of children from birth to young adulthood. There are many studies detailing the aging process for women, the effects of menopause, etc. However, there are relatively few studies detailing the male aging process, especially ones that focus on the implications for the harmonious succession of family firms.

Most studies of family conflict approach the difficulties from the view of the children; however, it must be recognized that parents also have "growing pains." Chapter Three draws heavily on the works of Dr. Daniel J. Levinson, author of *The Seasons of a Man's Life*, and Gail Sheehy's book, *Understanding Men's Passages*. Both are remarkable in their own ways and are well worth reading. Taken together, these books acknowledge that all men, family business owners included, follow fairly predictable evolutions as they age. The books detail some of the common struggles of men as they mature, allow us to see why family business succession can be such an emotional struggle, and help us understand why succession is a time of stress and conflict rather than triumph.

The failure of traditional family business advisors to recognize the trials of the male aging process and the dearth of family business literature of this "soft" subject and its implications for the business are simply more examples of why purely legal, technical and money solutions so frequently fail family businesses and their owners. Unless the human element and the family framework are taken into account, the picture of the business family is grossly incomplete.

Levinson made a remarkable discovery while researching the male aging process. He found that a man's life structure evolves through an orderly sequence through the adult years. It consists of alternately stable (structure building) and transitional (changing) periods. The stable periods typically last six to seven years; they don't last more than 10 years. Then, for various reasons, the life structure that forms the basis for stability comes into question by the individual and is modified. The transition period terminates the existing life structure and creates the opportunity for a new one. The task of the transition period is to reappraise the old, existing structure, to explore the possibilities for change, and to move toward the crucial choices that form the basis for the following stable period. Transitional periods lasted four to five years. A transition is a bridge, or boundary zone, between two stages of greater stability.

Levinson coined the phrase "life cycle" which has a distinctive meaning as it relates to the male aging process. It suggests that the life course has a particular character and follows a basic sequence. He found that the male life cycle follows a universal pattern subject to only modest individual variations.

With respect to family business owners, their creative drive to "birth" their enterprises and to generate life and being must be constrained by the inevitability of their aging and deaths. Recognizing the universal patterns of male aging can help the family business owner and his children choose the optimum time - and times precluded by transitional periods - for transferring management and ownership responsibilities to the next generation. Failure to recognize the optimum timing can doom even the most technically perfect succession plan and leave the family and advisors scratching their heads at why nothing resulted from all their time, effort, and money.

Overview of The Male Aging Process

Levinson identified four overlapping areas in the male life cycle consisting of about 25 years each in duration. The major developmental task of a structure building period is to make crucial choices to create a structure, to enrich the structure, and to pursue one's goals within it. These periods last about six to eight years. They are followed by transitional periods lasting four to five years.

Anticipating Sheehy's later work, Levinson referred to the "major seasons" of the life cycle. The eras are partially overlapping and the sequence goes as follows:

1. Childhood and Adolescence; age 0-22

2. Early Adulthood; age 17-45
3. Middle Adulthood; age 40-65
4. Late Adulthood; age 60-

It is important to note that stable and transition periods don't begin at precisely the same points for every individual; there is a range of variation around the average. He did find, however, that the variation is contained within very narrow limits - not more than five or six years. Much has been written about the first stage of the life cycle, childhood and adolescence. For the purpose of this book there is little need to review that era; our focus begins with the second era of the life cycle, early adulthood.

Early adulthood generally begins at 17 or 18 and ends at about 45. Levinson found that it is the most dramatic of all eras because the peak years of biological functioning fall within this period. At the back end of this period, the man passes 40, and a new season starts to manifest itself. At that point, the spring and summer of life has ended, and autumn is approaching.

The span of years between 20 and 40 is the era of greatest biological abundance and the greatest areas of contradiction and stress. At around 40, a crucial developmental change begins to occur. Early adulthood is coming to an end, and the Mid-Life Transition, which lasts from about 40 to 45, focuses the individual on the termination of early adulthood and the beginning of middle adulthood. While there is no single event that universally signals the end of early adulthood, the vast majority of individuals fall within a narrow four to six year transition window. During this period, the individual finds that his mental and physical energies begin to wane, but he also suffers less from the compulsive nature of ambition, lust, self-assertiveness, etc. During this period in which his elemental drives begin to soften, a man is able to get in touch with other sides of his psyche and begin to enrich his life in new ways. He begins to focus on his other qualities like passion, perspective, and wisdom.

Many men experience the change in their physical and mental

strengths as a fundamental threat to their existence, almost as if they were on the threshold of old age or even death. For many men, the Mid-Life Transition is rather mild. For others, it involves considerable turmoil and disruption, hence the term mid-life crisis. For some men, life in the middle years is unfortunately a process of gradual or rapid stagnation. Some men suffer from decline, and, as a result, decline is often seen as a normal part of middle age; this does not have to be the case. For some men, middle adulthood can be the fullest and most creative season in their life cycles. Levinson found that it is not possible to get through middle adulthood for men without having at least a moderate crisis in either the Mid-Life Transition (age 40) or the Age 50 Transition.

From about age 60 to 65, the Late Adult Transition terminates middle adulthood and creates a basis for late adulthood. It is a period of significant development and represents a major turning point in the life cycle. Even though the man is aging at this point, he has a real opportunity to do further developmental work and to create a more satisfying and fulfilling life. Whereas late adulthood has been seen as a period of decline and imminent death in the past, today many men find it to be a time of spiritual or relationship rejuvenation. For FBOs this time can be rich in fostering an environment for positive transition of the family company as well as creating more secure bonds in the second and third generations of the family and extended family. This is the era when the FBO will cast his legacy in concrete - for good or ill. Let's look at the individual seasons in more detail:

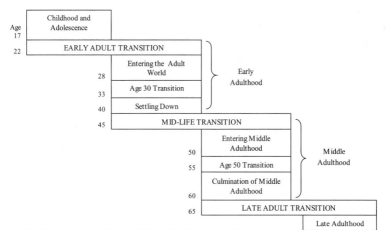

Source: *The Seasons of a Man's Life* by Dr. Donald J. Levinson

Early Adulthood

Levinson found that the process of entering into adulthood is far longer and more complicated than one might imagine. A young male needs about *15 years* to emerge from adolescence, find his place in adult society, and commit himself to a more stable life. There are three distinct phases that comprise this "novice phase" of Early Adult Transition. They are:

1. The Early Adult Transition (ages 17-22)
2. Entering the Adult World (ages 22-28)
3. The Age 30 Transition

The primary task of the novice phase is to make a place for the individual in the adult world. One must create a life structure for work and relationships that are appropriate to the adult world while simultaneously suitable to the individual. The first period of this novice phase, the Early Adult Transition, has two major tasks: the first is to leave the world of adolescence. The second is to make the first preliminary step into the adult world, to explore its possibilities, and to make and test some tentative choices before fully committing to adulthood.

Only 18% of the men in Levinson's study stayed close to their parents, personally and geographically, in their 20s. At the other extreme, 20% of the men of the group had major conflict with their parents - most often with their fathers - that went on for several years, and in some cases, permanently. This has significant implications for the family business. The family business demands that the individual stay close to his parents both personally and geographically if he enters the family business. A male who enters the family company right after college won't have the opportunity to create an independent identity separate from his parents. The fact that a significant number in Levinson's group had conflict with their fathers is especially troublesome for family companies. Most family companies report that there are periods of significant conflict and discord between fathers and sons during various stages of business and family development. The common recommendation of family business counselors is that the children - male and female - who propose to enter the family company do so only after three to five years of working for other companies. In light of Levinson's work, this is a smart precautionary step which allows individuals a chance to successfully navigate the Early Adult Transition without the added pressure of being the "boss' son" who was born with a silver spoon in his mouth and is now expected to succeed to the throne. The process of separation from parents continues over the life course; it is never completed. Therefore, a short, symbolic break during early adulthood can be critical in the satisfactory development of a person both as an individual and as a member of a business family.

The age 30 transition usually lasts about five years. A stressful transition was the rule more often than the exception in Levinson's study; about six out of 10 men go through a moderate or severe crisis in this period. Again, this has implications for children who enter the family business. In fact, some family business commentators have observed that members of younger generations should not be allowed to enter the business until age 30. By that point they have significant life and work experiences behind them before they bring their skills, talents, and abilities to the family company. While it may seem harsh to business families to preclude employment of children until they reach age 30, in light of Levinson's work it makes sense, especially for male children.

The end of the age 30 transition culminates in the settling down period. The important assignment in this area is to "settle for" a few key choices, to create a broader structure around the individual, to invest himself as fully as possible in the various components of this structure (work, family, community, friendships, etc.), and to pursue long range plans and goals. This is the era in which the individual begins to have a stronger sense of getting serious about his life and work. The settling down period begins at the end of the age 30 transition and ends at about age 40, just in time for the mid-life transition. During this period a man seeks to anchor his life more firmly in his occupation, his family, and his community. He begins to focus on advancing at work, using his skills more fully, becoming more creative, and contributing to society. The settling down period is the time for man to shape his dream, pursue his ambitions, and begin to develop his sense of heroic mission and who he would like to become. Contrary to conventional wisdom, Levinson observed that the 20s and 30s are simultaneously the most abundant and the *most stressful* decades in the male life cycle. The tasks of adaptation and development during this period are tremendously difficult.

Middle Adulthood

In middle adulthood, which begins around age 40, an individual can survey his past and make some judgment regarding his success or failure in meeting his stated or unstated goals. Often an individual looks at a key event that signals his affirmation or failure in the larger world. This "culminating event" can take on a magical quality in his quest for heroism. If the culminating event happens satisfactorily, he may believe he has truly succeeded and is assured of a happy future. If the culminating event turns out poorly, it may mean that he has failed in some sense, and he is found lacking personally, professionally, or both.

Levinson observed that a true mid-life transition can't really begin before age 38 or after age 43. It is within that narrow six-year window that the Mid-Life Transition has its onset. The most common age of onset is 40. The Mid-Life Transition is a bridge between early adulthood and middle adulthood. The person must work on three major tasks:

1. Terminate the era of early adulthood
2. Take the first steps toward middle adulthood
3. Deal with the polarities that are sources of deep division and conflict in life

Why does this mid-life transition begin around age 40? Levinson proposes an evolutionary answer. A man has reached his optimum size for mobility and survival at around age 18. If a primitive man had a son at age 18, his group had no more need for the father by the time he was 36. By that time, his son could hunt for food and take care of himself as a part of the group as well as or better than his father. The father became less valuable to the group because he could neither hunt nor fight as well as he once had. He became extraneous, and if he became sick or injured, he was a drag on the group and could easily be left behind to die. In other words, evolution dictated that a man would have his perfect physique and be at the height of his physical powers between the ages of 20 and 40. After 40, as decline set in, he was no longer as valuable to the group, and evolutionarily, he was superfluous. Levinson states that "our profound anxiety at passing forty reflects the ancient experience of the species; we still fear that life ends at forty."

A man around 40 reappraises his entire life up to that point. He tries to consider the direction he has taken and whether life will be better or worse in the future. The culminating event and other events surrounding it are markers as to whether or not life will get richer or poorer.

Carl Jung hypothesized that the Mid-Life Transition was an opportunity to improve as an individual. Prior to age 40, most individuals have only developed one or two of their four psychological functions (sensing, intuition, thought, and feeling). The age 40 transition and middle adulthood give an individual an opportunity to focus on and strengthen functions that were weak and lead a more balanced life.

Gail Sheehy observes that individuals arrive at the farthest reaches of their oppositeness between the sexes in the late thirties to early forties. She refers to this period as the "most distant poles of the Sexual Diamond." This is the culmination of differentiation which begins at puberty. After about 50, men and women move closer together and take on characteristics of the opposite gender. On the lower half of the diamond, men and women are becoming more alike rather than more different. At the mid-life transition, men and women are at their most opposite.

At age 40, a man may feel that the young man within him is

dying. By the late 30s and early 40s, a man has fallen well below his earlier peak levels of functioning. While the decline in functioning is normally quite moderate, often men experience the decline as catastrophic. They fear that they will lose all the youthful qualities that have made life worthwhile. The age 40 transition allows a man to grieve for the symbolic death of the youthful hero and begin to uncover new qualities he can develop heading into the next period of development. Levinson theorized that this painful recognition of a man's mortality stems from his wish for immortality. He wants to be assured of a permanent place in history or society. This painful transition is also a result of his fundamental love of life and his desire to see it continue.

Men achieve immortality, at least partly, through their professional and business accomplishments. Work, for men, is generally the most significant component of the life structure at mid-life and the major source of legacy. A depressing aspect of the mid-life transition is the realization that all previous successes were not as great as he once imagined. At best, the earlier successes form a foundation to the main body of work for the future, a foundation on which he can build to create his grand legacy and his sense of heroism. During the age 40 transition, a man has more inner freedom to be himself and is less obsessed with the passions of his ambition, lust, etc. The task of legacy building becomes more significant in a man's life than ever before.

Levinson found that the great majority of men - 80% in his study - have significant conflict and struggle during this period. Every aspect of their lives comes into question. Levinson said a "profound reappraisal of this kind cannot be a cool, intellectual process. It must involve emotional turmoil, despair, the sense of not knowing where to turn, or being stagnant and unable to move at all. A man in this state often makes false starts. He tentatively tests a variety of new choices, not only out of confusion or impulsiveness but, equally, out of a need to explore possibilities, to find out how it feels to engage in a particular love relationship, occupation, or solitary pursuit. Every genuine reappraisal must be *agonizing* because it challenges the illusions and vested interest on which the existing structure is based." The mid-life transition is a significant period of turmoil, reappraisal, and questioning for the majority of men.

The Struggle between Family Business Fathers and Sons

Just as the family business son comes to grips with who he is, where he is in life, and becomes eager to prove himself to his father, Dad begins to decline. This has implications for family business fathers and sons. Dad turns a little soft; he doesn't have the energy and stamina he once did. The son is, therefore, less able to lean on his father, and he is not ready to be leaned on himself. He may become irrationally angry at his Dad for getting soft at precisely the time he is ready to challenge Dad for supremacy. He may also feel subconsciously guilty for surpassing his dad in strength and vitality. It's a confusing period for fathers and sons.

The father of the mid-life son is battling his own inner demons. His aging begins to persuade him to relinquish his role as the omniscient, powerful master of the family business. While the son is struggling to master his own mid-life transition, Dad may be feeling weak relative to the other man, who happens to be his son, the father of his grandchildren, and the guarantor of his immortality as the new patriarch of the family business. Especially if the father has never felt confident about his own adult accomplishments, he'll find ways to undermine his son with subtle put-downs or outright criticism. Even more secure fathers may vacillate between withdrawing from the business and aggressively reasserting power. The vacillations may appear to be unpredictable and whimsical - and they are. The dad is struggling with his fear of letting go and what letting go ultimately means for the legacy he has worked so hard to create. The balance of power is shifting between the father and son, and it is a difficult and often painful transition for both. Sheehy goes as far as to say a "grown-up son makes his father feel redundant."

Irving Wallace commented that "a boy cannot become a man until his father dies, either literally or symbolically." This is an important concept in family businesses wherein Dad often has difficulty relinquishing authority to his child or children. As long as he holds on to the reins of power with an iron fist, his children cannot truly grow up. In order to let his children become as much as they can be, family business fathers need to step aside and let the children assert themselves. A fully self-actualized FBO learns to take gratification from his children's growing personal and professional powers and vicariously reconstitutes himself through their vigor and accomplishments.

Gail Sheehy states that "men are driven to prove themselves - perpetually - especially to other men. A man's greatest fear is of being dominated, or humiliated, by a stronger man in front of other men." How do men in middle life continue to demonstrate their manliness even as their physical strength wanes? This is a real question for family businesses. It is important to understand that many of the conflicts, which arise around succession issues, are not because Dad is stubborn or the son is overly aggressive. Some of these conflicts are a part of the natural evolution of men, and they're beyond the control of the family. The son is beset by fears that cannot accomplish as much as his father did before him. The father is beset by fears that the children will somehow damage his legacy and pull the rug of financial security out from under him. It is a period of uncertainty and trepidation on both sides.

The issue of earning Dad's blessing is never far from the surface. To a son working in a family business, nothing is more important than the knowledge that Dad approves of him and has given his blessing. Money, power, titles.... none mean as much to a son as hearing Dad say, "I'm proud of you. You are an outstanding person." The family business dad is a hero to his children as well as his employees and the community; nothing is more important than having the approval of that hero. However, the approval process is complicated by the competition which exists between fathers and sons. Many entrepreneurial parents have difficulty expressing affection and praise to anyone; it simply isn't their nature.

Fathers are often reluctant to tell sons how proud they are of them believing that too much praise might spoil the child or cause him to ease up. Quite the opposite is true; when family business sons no longer have to worry about whether or not Dad approves of them, they're finally free to focus on other, more important issues. Relations in the family become smoother, family gatherings become more pleasant, and the business operates better than ever before. Understanding the need for approval and the emotions involved in seeking Dad's blessing can be critical in making the business family more effective.

Middle Adulthood after the Mid-Life Transition

At around age 45 the developmental tasks for men change. The period after the Mid-Life Transition is devoted to starting a new era. Men become concerned about a wide menu of subjects they have never faced. Among them are aging, the loss of physical strength, losing parents, questioning the security of careers, questioning whether they will be closer to their children in the future, financial insecurity, etc. An individual may trapped by the overwhelming responsibilities of owning and operating a successful family business. He may have a fear that, if something happens to him or his health, he could lose the dream - the magnificent obsession that he brought to life. He may feel that all the comforts and financial security that accrued as a successful FBO could be lost, and the time and effort that it would take to replace the comfort and security would be crushing. His whole identity is tied up in the family business and the status it has bestowed upon him. If he lets go of what he has built, even a little bit, what would happen to him?

However, in this second adulthood (as Gail Sheehy calls it), family business owners can learn that satisfaction in life is not the result of "racking up points on a single scoreboard. There are many different ways to keep score - as father, husband, friend, mentor, philanthropist, teacher, etc. Until about age 45, most men are so focused on getting ahead and staying there that they usually miss the clear signals that could prepare them for a satisfying, fulfilling strategy for their later years."

Sheehy refers to the "Age of Mastery," a whole new stage that opens up in the middle of life between the ages of 45 and 60. Passing from first to second adulthood and into the age of mastery can transform the idea of power for family business owners. Sheehy writes that the mid-point of adulthood is no longer about age 40; it is more like age 50. She suggests that the "fearless fifties" offer possibilities that previous generations couldn't even imagine. Today's family business owners can tap into new sources of meaning and purpose to propel themselves into their later years. However, they need to make a conscious decision to redirect their lives before a catastrophic event - like a heart attack or a period of deep despondency - makes their decision for them. They need to plan to win in their later years, and they need to have the will to *prepare* to win by replacing the things that advancing age takes away.

Late Adult Transition

In the early 60s, middle adulthood comes to an end, and the period of late adulthood begins. Now more than ever, this period of life is a distinctive and fulfilling season of life rather than a period of decline and decay. It lasts from about 60 to 85. For the first time, events like illness or retirement may signal the end of a given period and offer a direction for the coming transition.

At around 60, the reality of bodily decline begins to set in. Mental and physical changes intensify a man's experience of his aging and mortality. They remind him that he is moving from middle age to old age. For the first time, the FBO's friends, colleagues, and loved ones are facing serious illnesses or even death. The FBO himself is likely to have at least one major illness or other physical or mental problems. Every man in the late adult transition must face a decline or loss of some of his middle adult powers.

What does it mean to an FBO to turn 60 and feel that old age is staring him in the face? The FBO fears that the youth within him is dying and that he'll survive for a relatively brief and undignified old age. He finds that he cannot always occupy center stage in his world. His declining mental and physical powers require that he reduce some of the massive responsibilities that he has taken on over the years. He must change his relationship with his company, his family, and his employees. Moving out of the limelight is traumatic and anxious for the family business owner. He may find that when someone from the company is called for a quote for the local newspaper, it is his son that they phone and not him. He may no longer be perceived in the community as the dominant force in the family company; he is now a part of the grandparent generation.

Family business fathers fight the late adult transition bitterly. Levinson writes, "if he does not give up his authority, he is likely to become a tyrannical ruler - despotic, unwise, unloved, and unloving - and his adult offspring may become puerile adults unable to love him or themselves. In his work life, too, there will be serious difficulties if a man holds a position of formal authority beyond age sixty-five or seventy. If he does so, he is "out of phase" with his own generation, and he is in conflict with the generation in middle adulthood who need to assume greater responsibilities."

This doesn't mean that the FBO doesn't have something to offer; he does. However, he shouldn't hold on to absolute authority in his family enterprise because of the damage it can do currently (to the self-esteem of the succeeding generation) and in the future (when, ultimately, that generation must step up to the plate with two out in the bottom of the ninth). In other words, an FBO who is desperately hanging on to the reins of power cannot simultaneously train his successors to do the jobs required of them. The children, who are probably in middle adulthood, suffer from their powerlessness and lack of challenge. Even the grandchildren can suffer! They may be deprived of the moral authority and positive role models they need from their parents.

The proper role for the senior FBO is to "refocus" his energies. He can still be valuable to the company he created, but he needs to demonstrate his value in different ways. He needs to be a mentor and a teacher rather than a doer and decision maker. He can become an ambassador for his company, to the community, to his trade association, or to the philanthropic world. He can function as a consultant to the management of his company without engaging in direct day-to-day decision making. He can pursue some of the dreams he had when he was younger but never had time for. He can even start new companies or spin-off divisions to focus on new business opportunities. In short, the period of refocusing can be a tremendous boon to the FBO and the succeeding generations.

The period of late, late adulthood comes around the age of 80. Men who reach this age are suffering from various declines in bodily function and at least one severe illness. By this time, the life structure is small in terms of territory and other relationships. A preoccupation with immediate comfort and bodily needs emerges. Life in this late era may begin to lose meaning. A man at this stage in life must begin to reconcile himself to the fact that he is, in fact, dying. With modern advances in health, nutrition, exercise, and medical science, the rate of dying is significantly different today from a generation ago. However, a man who is 80 or above simply doesn't have much more time. That does not mean that the FBO can't continue to add meaning and richness to his life and the lives of others. He may set a strong example of wisdom and positive influence. Sheehy writes about a Harvard study that found that the emotional health of men over 65 wasn't grounded in a happy childhood or success in their careers. Rather, it was those who had developed resilience to absorb life's shocks and conflicts who were best able to enjoy their later years. The most valuable asset they gained over time was the self-awareness to control their first impulses and to respond in a calm, measured way to stimuli. The greatest fear of old age is the fear of irrelevance. The major concerns of late, late adulthood are:

1. How will I be remembered?
2. What will my life mean to my family?
3. Is it too late to create more meaning in my life in the time I have left?

Men versus Women

Sheehy writes, "men don't understand women, but at least they know it. Women don't understand men, but they don't know it." The problem as it relates to family businesses, and FBOs in particular, is that as men age they have a deeper need to be understood by their mates; there is a period of "gender crossover." In their 50s to mid-60s, men begin to warm up, mellow, and desire more intimate relationships with their wives, children, and friends. As they age, men continue to identify with being male, but they no longer need to prove themselves by physical or sexual conquests.

Just as the FBO gets more in touch with his feelings and spends more time relaxing, his wife, perhaps for the first time, has the freedom and energy to pursue some of her dreams she put on hold in favor of children, hearth, and home. Married women who are roughly the same age and who are in the same developmental stages as their mates are often out of rhythm with each other. When healthy, educated women reach their 50s, they generally feel energized. They have freedoms which they never had before. They begin to look for positive changes, develop careers, and often initiate separate vocational lives from their mates. Men, on the other hand, are much needier and more dependent at this stage of life. It may be said that they suffer from "separation anxiety" as the spouse begins to assert more of herself into the relationship. Sheehy found that *100% of the men in her study* said their spouses were their primary sources of intimacy and comfort. Men in this crossover stage can become threatened that they are less needed by the women in their lives.

Gender crossover can escalate into a crisis when the man is not self-actualized or believes the myth that men must dictate and dominate in all spheres of the marriage relationship. He'll have trouble watching his wife develop and come into her own just as he is ready to spend more time at home and away from the office. Instead of being welcomed home and congratulated for his migration towards his feelings, the FBO is confused and dumbfounded by the fact that his presence isn't what his wife wants after all! Not only does he have separation anxiety from the departure from his business - his first born child and greatest creation - he has separation anxiety at home because his emotional anchor has developed a need to exercise her creative ambition outside the home.

Men and women are vastly different in the way they approach old age. The fact that the FBO's spouse doesn't accept the role of omnipresent, doting, appreciative wife just at the time when he has realized he has to begin the process of withdrawal from the business can hit the FBO like a ton of bricks. Gender crossover issues and the spouse's career ambitions can leave the FBO floundering with both his work and home roles confused and, suddenly, threatening. Children in family businesses can be caught in the middle. They'd like to see Dad relax and reap some of the benefits of his hard work. They would also like more responsibility and the chance to show what they can do in the business. However, due to his role confusion at home, the FBO finds it harder than ever to give up the one constant he still has, his heroic presence in his company.

Preparing for the Inevitable - Anticipating and Managing Change During the Male Aging Process

Sheehy concludes that men today are having a harder time making a satisfying transition in the second half of their lives. She also observes that, although we all know change is inevitable, men run headlong into change like it is a brick wall. She theorizes that if they knew better what to expect, they could anticipate and make changes with greater ease.

By middle age, the man's body doesn't bounce back from physical exertion the way it once did. Women have menopause, a universal sign that signals the first adulthood is over and the time for second adulthood is nearing. For men, this change is more subtle and, therefore, challenging. There is no physical or spiritual demarcation point. There are, however, significant exit events:

1. Death of a parent
2. Divorce
3. Loss of a self-defining job
4. Death of a peer
5. Death of a mentor
6. Children leaving home

These are all among the terrible, irreconcilable losses in life. Men don't associate change with growth; they generally associate change with loss or being forced to give up something. Change isn't seen as a positive part of the growth process on the road to new, exciting challenges.

Family business owners are particularly guilty of managing their personal changes poorly. Because family business owners define themselves largely by their work, they are frightened by the prospect of what they will do when the work stops. The higher the status embodied in one's work, the steeper the slide to anonymity. John Medlin, the former CEO of Wachovia Bank, confided to Family Business Institute co-founder Tom Campbell that the day he retired he went from being "who's who" to "who's he?" It's a farther fall for someone at the top of the pyramid than it is for someone at the bottom. Men ironically become vulnerable when their positions bestow upon them great power and influence over others. They think that retirement equals death; they watch those who have retired wither away and die with both disdain and trepidation. Their egos, deservedly large after a lifetime of triumph over adversity, won't allow them to get out of their own way and adapt rather than pushing ever forward.

Men have different coping mechanisms for dealing with emotional conflict than women. The most common ways that men cope with disputes are withdrawing and withholding. They simply get out of the situation and "hole up." They have an exaggerated physical reaction to stress relative to women. Men's bodies produce higher quantities of stress chemicals and higher blood pressure than women's do in reaction to sudden danger. Men also tend to hold on to anger longer than women. It is said that men remain cool under pressure. However, researchers have found that remaining cool under pressure does not mean their bodies remain cool. Rather it means that they are able to disconnect emotionally while the body retains its "fight or flight" posture in preparation for handling physical distress. This physical reaction also helps explain why fathers and sons in family businesses don't communicate better! The nature for males is to flee from confrontation rather than to engage in healthy conflict resolution. Sheehy writes that physiological change even goes so far as to render the man *unable to hear* what his opponent is saying. Evolution has simply not equipped us for modern methods of dealing with emotional stress and conflict. That is why conflict resolution and positive communication skills must be taught to family business families rather than relying solely on love and a desire for harmony in a family to keep the lid on crisis.

Conclusion

Chapter Three has shown that undertaking family business succession, exit strategy, organizational development, or estate planning without understanding the ages and stages of the family members involved is a prescription for failure. The Mid-Life Transition begins a second adulthood for men. Their physical strength is declining just as they are reaching their fullest potential as leaders. How they cope with the changes nature forces upon them is the test that determines their courage or cowardliness. They face mounting exit events and possibly their own first physical infirmities. Since these changes are going to come, FBOs must anticipate and prepare for them.

An important task for men in late adulthood is to release the tyranny of putting out fires every day and to begin to dream about their families, companies, and communities. The FBO is the master architect of our business culture, and designing a second life which can give him freedom and meaning is the key to creating an enduring legacy.

CHAPTER FOUR

FAMILY BUSINESS INFLUENCES AND DECISION-MAKING

PRESCRIPTION: Since FAMILY is the critical part of the family business enterprise; be aware of the nature of changing families and develop decision-making systems to support both the family and the business.

Family business owners often lament that they "get stuck" when doing planning because they cannot come to grips with all the contingent (and moving) parts of their families, the employees who make up the business family, the ownership of their firms, and the management of their companies. Because one or another of the myriad moving parts is or becomes problematic, the entire planning process comes to a halt. Problems are addressed or, more likely, ignored while everyone hopes they will fix themselves. Doing strategic, life-giving planning is postponed until another day.

Professionals, bankers, insurance agents, and other advisors often wonder why their beautifully crafted, technically marvelous business and estate plans go unimplemented and end up on a shelf gathering dust. Family members, especially the children who are management employees, become frustrated at the "hurry up and wait" nature of the strategic planning process. In short, the succession and estate planning process becomes a testy and uncomfortable time for everyone involved. No wonder so many FBOs and their families throw up their hands in frustration and ignore the necessities altogether.

Legal, technical, and money solutions to family business problems *are wrong* unless the family issues are addressed *first*. Proper family business planning requires an integrated approach that incorporates a deep understanding of the nature of families that work together as well as good technical skills. Only by viewing each family business system as an integrated whole can one have true insight into successfully resolving sticky business and/or family issues.

There is a set of guidelines successfully used by top family business consultants. The guidelines form a basic philosophy of how satisfying results can be reached and how successful, win-win strategies can serve the interests of all parties:

1. The perspectives of all business family members and stake holders must be taken into account in order to develop a balanced approach and win-win solutions for all involved.
2. It is important to view the business family and the family

business as a complex system of interlocking relationships which are simultaneously independent and interdependent.

3. Communication throughout the business family system is essential and often must be facilitated by an independent, objective third party.

It is exceedingly rare to find systems in which families, management, and power are synchronized and balanced. The rule rather than the exception is that each of the family business dimensions is slightly out of phase with the others. One of the most common sources of intrigue in family companies is the conflict between individuals at different life stages over business management styles and appetites for business risk. A real life example will help illustrate this problem.

Tom Campbell spent 24 years in business with his father, mother, and two brothers. When Tom was in his forties, his dad was in his 70s. They were in the radio business which was in a period of rapidly appreciating business value. Referring to Figure One, Tom's (Junior Generation) appetite for risk was on the increase. He wanted to make his mark on the radio world by acquiring more properties. His father, Hartwell (Senior Generation), on the other hand, had had more than his share of risk over his many years in broadcasting and was ready to slow down and take life a little easier. As long as the two individuals were on the far left side of the equilibrium point, harmony was the rule. After the risk appetites for the two had passed beyond the initial stages, conflict was the result. In other words, Tom still wanted to conquer the radio world while his father had fought quite enough battles and was much more interested in maintaining territory rather than conquering new ground. Due to the different growth philosophies, they mutually decided to sell their various holdings and move in different directions. For this business family, selling the company was the right thing to do to preserve their family relationship.

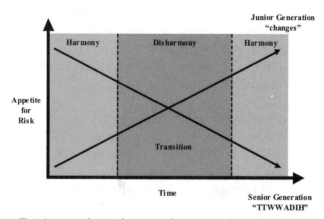

Tom's experience is not unique. As time goes by and the second generation matures and learns the family business, temperatures rise as new and old ways compete. The younger generation advocates change and evolution while the older generation advocates TTWWADIH (that's the way we've always done it here). The resulting competition for who will lead, manage, and own the business (a conflict as old as Oedipus) results in an often prolonged period of disharmony, frustration, and uncertainty.

Eventually, either willingly or unwillingly, the senior generation departs and the junior generation is free to run the business as he sees fit - until the next generation of change agents come along in the form of siblings or the third wave of family business offspring.

The Business Family

Kelin Gersick, John Davis, Ivan Lansberg, and Marion M. Hampton in their book *Generation To Generation*, cite the work of Dave and John Aldous who wrote a wonderful description of the nature of families:

> *The nuclear family is perhaps more subject to orgational instability than other organizations because of its rapily*

changing age composition and frequently changing plurality patterns. Its leaders are two relatively inexperienced amateurs in the roles of spouse and parent. They must work with a succession of followers having few skills and lacking judgment under conditions that appear never to remain stable enough, long enough, to allow for organization. The family has hardly . established one set of relations based on mutual, normative expectations and agreements when some child begins demanding a reinterpretation of the rights and duties built into his roles. Yet, despite these disruptive factors which are a part of its standardoperating procedures, the family somehow, in a majority of cases, manages to maintain the structured interaction patterns that enable it to continue as an entity.

Families proceed through evolutionary life cycles in only one direction. Aging is a fact of life and cannot be avoided by even the most determined family. As children age, the amount of day-to-day contact between generations gradually diminishes. In a typical family, by the time children have reached their early 20s, contact may be sporadic to non-existent. In business families, by contrast, there is *more* contact between family members after the early 20s. Working side-by-side in the family enterprise requires some level of interaction on a virtually daily basis. This, of course, is true for employee family members; non-employee family members fit more closely with the standard family model of diminishing contact over time.

Family theorists have developed a scale for describing the level of contact and togetherness in families. The continuum may be called the enmeshment-disengagement scale. The **interdependent/enmeshed family** tends to be very sensitive to one another's needs and preferences. They rely on the opinions of other family members to guide their behavior. They make few personal or family decisions without consulting other family members and coming to a type of consensus.

There is a remarkable amount of decision-making uniformity. Every family member feels involved in the group and has a stake in decision-making. In fact, some interdependent/enmeshed families have a type of "family veto power." If *all* family members do not unanimously agree on a decision, the decision either won't be made or one dissenting voice will carry the day. Even in a situation where the majority of family members agree that a decision must be made, a lone dissenting voice often prevails in the elusive pursuit of family harmony. This phenomenon occurs in family businesses with remarkable frequency in spite of the knowledge of the majority that changes or decisions must be made for the good of the business and the family.

The **independent/disengaged family** varies greatly from the interdependent/enmeshed family. While people in these types of families have the same last name and the same place of origin, they don't have much else in common. They have very different preferences, personal goals, and, sometimes, business goals. Each individual marches to the beat of a different drummer, has his own set of friends outside the family, and pursues his own extracurricular activities independent of the rest of the family. Other than a basic skeleton of rules necessary to maintain some semblance of discipline in the family enterprise, there is little structure in this group; internal communication is weak. There is a strong streak of competitiveness in the group. Decisions are often made by one member of the group without consulting the thoughts and feelings of others or considering the consequences the decisions might have on them. Consensus is rarely sought and rarely achieved.

The **coherent family** tries to reach balance and consensus in making both family and business decisions. They are neither too enmeshed nor too disengaged. They are effective as individuals in their interactions with people outside the family system and effective as a group. There are rules and structures in place; management is not heavy handed or autocratic. There is a good balance in individual pursuits, decision making, group harmony, and communication.

Family businesses tend to be on the enmeshed/interdependent

side of the scale. This may be why it is common in business families to find an "escape artist" who feels suffocated by the enmeshed style of the family and looks for an opportunity to leave the family business system, set out on her own, and make her own way in the world independent of the smothering environment of the interdependent family.

Psychiatrists refer to a process called individuation as children strive to separate themselves from their families. Everyone goes through the process of individuation and tries to develop a sense of identity independent of other family members. People who have achieved individuation are healthy and well balanced individuals. They are neither obsessed with pleasing other people, nor are they crushed by constructive criticism. They care about others and society, but they are not so focused on pleasing that they ignore their own needs. Those who are not well individuated tend to overreact to input from relatives. They are hypersensitive when it comes to criticism and take any slight personally. Because of the prolonged close contact of the business family, individuation is a difficult process for family business members. The lack of successful individuation can often lead to conflict in the business due to hypersensitivity and the lack of clear boundaries between "your turf and mine." It takes a healthy and self-actualized person to react constructively to the interpersonal demands of family businesses without being overly sensitive or overly aloof.

Birth order is an interesting phenomenon in the family enterprise. Recent research of birth order provides new insights on why children from the same household can be so different. Author Frank Sulloway, in his book *Born To Rebel; Birth Order, Family Dynamics, and Creative Lives*, compiled research on more than six thousand people. He found that firstborn children from different families are often more alike than siblings from the same family. Firstborn children are usually authoritarian, defenders of the status quo, and are more conservative than their later born siblings. They are generally more comfortable in take charge situations than younger siblings. They are generally more conscientious, responsible, more worried, and more anxious about problems beyond their control. By way of contrast, laterborn children are inclined to be more liberal and open minded in their thinking. They tend to accept new ideas more readily than first born children. Sulloway also found that sibling differences often outweigh gender differences. Firstborn women can be as conservative as their firstborn male counterparts. A firstborn, whether male or female, is a more likely candidate to become a meticulous mechanical engineer than a laterborn child.

Children from the same parents are raised, in effect, by different parents. Between the birth of the first child and the last, especially if there are many years in between, the parents change economically, physically, and psychologically. A child's place in the birth order is a major influence on his experience of childhood. Parents are most anxious and attentive when raising their first child. By the time other children come along, they are more relaxed and experienced. The inescapable conclusion is that many factors, including child rearing, change parents. For example, when there is a gap of six or more years, a younger child may enjoy the parents' full attention and grow up as the second "oldest child."

Sulloway also theorizes that primogeniture is dead. Business succession planning requires objective assessment of the leadership abilities, historical performance, temperament, and other factors of the candidates. The stage of the family company in the business life cycle calls for skill sets and personality traits which may or not be associated with oldest sons. Family companies are becoming meritocracies where performance is more vital than birth order. Simply because one child was born a few years before another does not make him the right choice for CEO.

Middle children have a unique place. They are neither first nor last, tallest nor smallest, etc. They have difficulty getting recognition. Since they tend to not get special emphasis in the context of the family, they tend to either look outside the family structure for recognition or exert extraordinary demands for recognition within the family. They can become very effective negotiators as adults because they had to negotiate to get anything as children. Some psychologists theorize that middle children ultimately tend to be better adjusted than children in other birth positions.

In addition to birth order, the sex mix in a family can have a direct impact. People who grow up in families with both boys and girls learn to live and share intimacy with members of the opposite sex. Those who grow up in single sex households have not shared home life with the opposite sex and generally are not as strong in relating to members of the other gender. David Bork, in *Family Business, Risky Business*, writes about an analysis of over three thousand marriages which were assigned to three types of relationships: complementary, non-complementary, and doubly non-complementary. In complementary relationships, there was no conflict over rank in birth order and each partner in the marriage had an opposite sex sibling. There were no divorces among couples having complementary relationships in this study.

In non-complementary relationships there was a conflict of either birth order or sex. If the conflict is over birth order and, for example, two oldest children marry, there are issues over control. If the conflict is over sex mix, the partners have difficulty relating to the opposite sex because neither had an opposite sex sibling in the household of origin.

The doubly non-complementary relationship features a conflict over both birth order and sex. For example, a marriage between an oldest brother of three brothers and oldest sister of three sisters is a doubly non-complementary relationship. These couples have issues over control since both are the oldest and attempt to take charge and are not skilled in sharing intimacy in living arrangements with members of the opposite sex. The divorce rate in doubly non-complementary marriages was twice that of the study sample.

There are other factors that affect the business family and its relationships. Sibling rivalry is one of those issues. In family businesses, there are generally three types of children. The first is the defiant child who is determined to be beat the family business entrepreneur at his own game. His attitude is "I'll show you old man. I can be better than you, and I'm going to prove it." He competes with his siblings as well as his father. Frequent disagreements and arguments are the norm, generally over disputed methods to reach the same goal. The defiant child wants to demonstrate leadership and ability by showing Dad and siblings new ways to do things while Dad often sees the child as impudent, wanting to change the way things have worked successfully for many years. Sometimes Dad even thinks the child is trying to undermine his authority. Often there is so much competitive drive in Dad that he cannot allow anyone, even his own son, to best him. There is a competition between entrepreneurs, siblings, and defiant children, and all feel only one of them can win. This can be a dangerous sport and must be recognized for what it is before relationships become so strained that they are damaged beyond repair.

The second approach for children to deal with sibling rivalry is to become the "compliant child." The compliant child is willing to do whatever Dad wants even if the child doesn't think it is right. The logic is that if the child does his best to do what Dad wants, surely he will be seen as a worthy child who deserves the blessing and approval of his parents and siblings. This could be very frustrating for a child who seldom feels personal growth and often feels like a doormat. Dad might even privately express concern that the child is not demonstrating any leadership in the business. Sometimes the only way for a child to work in a domineering family company is to become compliant, but it generally isn't healthy for the business or the child.

The third type of child in family businesses is the "escape artist." This child, for whatever reason, decides he can't compete with his father and siblings in the family business arena, so he finds a field in which he can compete and excel. The thinking is that if he can show Dad how great he has become in his own area of expertise, Dad will approve and shower his blessing on him. The escape artist talks about how great it is not to be in the business, but secretly he still craves the approval of his father and the other family members.

Another type of sibling rivalry that occurs in family businesses is between employee children and non-employee children. Those who are non-employees may feel that they get less attention, status, and family identity than those who are employed. Employee children may become frustrated with their non-employee siblings because they feel the non-employee children get a "free ride" with respect to the family wealth, and they are scrutinized far less intensely because of their relative remoteness.

Still another source of intrigue in family businesses is the relationship between birth families and in-laws. In-laws in family companies often wear black hats and are perceived by members of the birth family to be agitators and interlopers. Family business in-laws may come to resent each other because of fears that their spouses may somehow be put at a disadvantage in the family business relative to their siblings. While family business in-laws often get a bad rap, they often turn out to be the most well adjusted and capable members of subsequent generations in business families.

Most of the conflict relating to enmeshment, disengagement, individuation, birth order, sex mix, sibling rivalry, etc., are communication issues. The greatest tool for improving and solidifying business family communications is the Family Council which we will explore in greater detail in Chapter Seven. Another *communication issue* unique to family enterprises is decision making - or the lack thereof!

The Paradox of Family Business Decision-Making

The conventional wisdom with regard to family businesses is that one of the advantages they have over their larger competitors is that they're smaller and more nimble and are, therefore, capable of making faster, better business decisions. After observing business families attempting to make decisions over the years, we'd like to respectfully challenge the conventional wisdom. One caveat: let's stipulate that, when it comes to operations, family businesses typically do have excellent decision-making. Because of the depth of their experience in their particular field, and the fact they've specialized in their industry over one or more generations, they are capable of making speedy decisions when it comes to operations. When it comes to other areas - particularly strategy and long-term direction for the family business - their decision-making abilities erode significantly.

Most family businesses still in the first generation have one primary decision maker who happens to be both owner and general manager of the enterprise. First generation family business owners are often like battlefield generals issuing directives left and right and watching lower ranked soldiers execute their decisions. However, when the founder has aged and the second generation enters the business in a significant management role, big picture decision-making gets bogged down and, as dad ages further, grinds almost to a halt.

Family businesses that are beyond the peak earning years of the founding generation make strategic family business decisions by "consensus." After many years, we still are not certain exactly what consensus means in the context of family companies. As near as we can determine, consensus decision-making in family businesses really means *unanimous* decision-making. Remember what Margaret Thatcher said about consensus decision-making: "Consensus is the *absence* of leadership." When family businesses say they make decisions by consensus, what they really mean is that unanimity is required; this gives effective veto power to anyone who dissents from a group decision. Think about how destructive this might be for family businesses trying to make important, strategic, long term decisions that relate to the future health and vitality of their company!

Here's an example. A family business is populated by five family members: Dad, the founder, age 80, Mom, age 77, the oldest son, age 50, who is the president of the company, the next son, age 48, who is a vice president, and the youngest child, a daughter, age 46, who is also a vice president. The family has been considering for several years some strategic decisions that could modernize the business and allow them to resume faster growth. Most of the five family members are either very enthusiastic or somewhat enthusiastic about the idea. The difficulty is that the second son, the vice president of operations, is not enthusiastic about the proposed changes at all, and has made his displeasure known through several heated exchanges. Given the fact that 80% of the family members are on board for the proposed changes, what is this family in business likely to do?

The answer seems simple. Most laymen would look at this situation and say because four of the five stakeholders have made themselves clear that the project should be a go, the decision is a no brainer. However, when it comes to the paradox of family business decision-making, odds are that this family will **NOT** move forward with any strategic initiative - at least in the short run.

Why is this phenomenon so prevalent in family businesses? Why would people endowed with good minds and common sense give any one person in a group of five effective veto power over any decision that the group would likely make?

In the family example above, the reason they won't move forward with their strategic plans is they don't want to upset the child who is vice president of operations. In their pursuit of family harmony, most families determine that it's not in their interest from a harmony perspective to upset anyone in the family at any time. While this may seem unrealistic, it's common behavior. Therefore, four people out of five will put their dreams and aspirations on hold in order to avoid stepping on the toes of the one dissenter. In order to preserve family harmony and to avoid conflict, veto power is handed out to anyone who diverges from the wishes of the larger group.

The irony is that, if this dissenter continues to veto family business initiatives, he will create much greater conflict than would have been experienced otherwise. As the dissenter's power grows and he becomes the de facto leader of the company through his willingness to use his veto power, resentment and frustration build in the other members of the group. The issue is that this convoluted effort to preserve family harmony actually undermines good relations over time by allowing an imbalance of power to accrue to anyone who chooses to prevent unanimity!

This is a shortsighted strategy for preserving family business harmony and results in increased family business conflict and disharmony over time if it's allowed to take place repeatedly. This is only a strategy for *deferring* conflict, not for dealing with it constructively.

In second or subsequent generation family businesses, the way decisions are made depends on the management style of the company leader(s). There are three different decision-making styles depending on the leader's business philosophy. The first is the **dominant sibling** or first **among equals** leadership style. This is typified by one sibling who takes on the founder or senior generation's role of ultimate authority and decision-making. Whether or not this individual owns majority control of the shares of the enterprise, he behaves and makes decisions as if he does; he might be described as a benevolent dictator. For siblings or cousins who work in the business, there may be some resentment: "she makes all the decisions without consulting me..." The resentment on the part of the dominant sibling is that, "I do all the work, but I have to share the equity growth with my siblings who barely pull their weight..." Both sides experience unfairness in the situation.

The second type of sibling relationship might be called **détente** or **M.A.D.** (mutually assured destruction). The situation is typified by each sibling in the business having her own turf. A sibling hoards information to consolidate her power and position within her area of responsibility. She exercises unilateral authority and makes decisions within her sphere of influence. Family business siblings often discuss this type of arrangement by saying, "We get along great. She has her role, I have mine, and we don't really overlap."

While this may seem idyllic, there are problems. There's generally a lack of common vision; for example, if one sibling runs sales and the other runs fulfillment, the departments may suffer from a lack of coordination and may find themselves competing with each other. There's also jealousy over which department adds more to the company's success. Each sibling he does all the work while the other has all the fun. The sales sibling says, "I could sell twice as much, but production can't keep up with delivery and service, so why should I try?" Production has similar criticism for sales. Both siblings think that the situation is inherently unfair; however, venturing into the turf of the other sibling is the same as flinging down the gauntlet and preparing for war.

The third type of sibling decision-making style is the Team or

Collaborative style. It's typified by frequent meetings, conversations, emails, and retreats. There's participative management with sharing of all vital company information. There are shared visions among the siblings or cousins for what the company is, what it's going to be, and what the company represents to the family.

The team/collaborative approach isn't without its issues, however. It's harder and may take longer to make decisions. It requires advance planning, preparation, and scheduling. It can also cause uncomfortable issues to be raised which, as we've seen, is something to be avoided at all cost in many family companies.

If the family company uses the dominant sibling or the détente style over long periods of time, they'll experience the following effects:

- Short term harmony (perhaps), but long term disharmony
- Stagnation
- Factionalization
- Frustration
- Pessimism
- Constriction of vision which leads to seeing only negative outcomes for the family or business future
- Explosion

What should second or subsequent generation family companies do when faced with group decisions and the absence of unanimous agreement? There are several steps:

1. Recognize that not making a decision is, in fact, a decision.
2. Embrace change. It's inevitable, cannot be halted, and is usually necessary for both family and business. Once people accept the change as simply a fact of life, it somehow ceases to be as threatening and problematic.
3. Take steps to understand yourself and your other family members better. There are many instruments available to assess your own personality as well as those of the people you

work and live with. Use them to learn to communicate better.

4. Determine in advance what you as a family and a business will do in the absence of unanimity, ties, or deadlocks on decisions. Define what decisions require what levels of decision-making. Which can be made unilaterally by family members or managers? What decisions need consultation? With whom? At what levels? Who (if anyone) has veto power? When? By what virtue? What decisions require a vote? What decisions require a majority vote, super majority vote, or a unanimous vote? What's the voting procedure: is it one person, one vote? Is it unequal weighting for the votes of some people? Is there a consensus or rating voting system that you can employ?

5. Resolve the decision-making conflicts; don't avoid them! While it might not make sense to force a decision immediately (let's face it, sometimes sleeping on an issue for a week or two is a good way to gain greater perspective), it doesn't mean you should avoid making decisions altogether. Conflict resolution leading to effective decision-making is healthy for families and businesses. Successful family businesses take action steps to make real, thoughtful decisions. Making no decision at all is still a decision, and the resulting lack of resolve and clarity penalizes a family business in the long run.

Conclusion: Can Your Family Business Be Truly Healthy If Your Business Family Is Not?

The question above is not rhetorical. Each family needs to address this question in its own way and come to a conclusion. Does the family exist to serve the business or does the business exist to serve the family? It is possible to have a strong management team and a financially successful company without effective, loving family relationships. However, if the family business is a substitute for a strong family, ultimately tensions, intrigues, and squabbling will sink not only the family but also the company which it spawned. It is critical that families have effective, open, supportive, loving communication to improve the bonds of family which are so vital to the long term success and stability of family enterprises. Families need to have a clear sense of their purposes. Steven Covey, in *The Seven Habits Of Highly Effective Families*, says that a Family Mission Statement is the single most important guiding force in developing a family purpose. Families should also have effective methods for communication and decision-making. Since informality abounds in family businesses, creating a structured, formal format for family communication goes a long way toward allowing people to express their feelings, anxieties, desires, and ambitions regularly and without filtering.

The business needs several prescriptions in order to go forward. First, the business needs a clear vision of what it should look like. Second, there must be clear roles and responsibilities defined for each member of the management team. Third, there must be specific rules of entry for members of the family who wish employment in the family enterprise. Fourth, there must be formal meetings on the operation of the company as well as formal meetings on relationships to improve the communication of key managers and to monitor adherence of the management team to the business plan and business vision. Often it is important to have outsiders facilitate both the family and the business meetings in order to make them effective and to bring freshness and energy to meetings which can easily become humdrum and stale. Improved communication and decision-making in the family and the business can only help each achieve new levels of success.

CHAPTER FIVE

THE TEN MOST COMMON AND COSTLY ESTATE AND SUCCESSION MISTAKES MADE BY FAMILY BUSINESS OWNERS

PRESCRIPTION: Avoid the 10 most common estate and succession planning errors of family business owners. Any one of them could devastate your company, tear apart your family, or BOTH!

When asked about the family business's plan of succession and transition, most family firm owners say heartily, "I've been to my lawyer, and I've got it all taken care of!" Nothing could be further from the truth!

While there are some truly gifted family business planning attorneys, plans drafted by lawyers are usually tax wise, family foolish, and business foolish. When family business owners refer to their "succession plans," they are really referring to their drop-dead documents (wills, trusts, and other testamentary documents). Because they've spent time and often great deals of money to purchase these documents and engage in a planning process, legal documents provide for the *illusion* of transition or succession planning. They are, in reality, drop dead plans that do not begin to address the issue of "what if you live?" They're also top down plans which may not be consistent with the wishes of employee and/or non-employee children or employees of the family firm.

A survey by the University of Connecticut of 800 recently failed family companies found that the overwhelming reason why these firms ceased to exist was non-existent or inadequate planning. Off-the-shelf, technical solutions which work fine for a doctor, lawyer, or corporate executive will not work for a family company because of its unique overlap of the family, ownership of the business, and management of the business. The overlapping dynamics and relationships of the family enterprise are simply not adequately factored into the planning process.

Successful planning in a family company involves much more than legal and technical documents. The planning must involve every stakeholder in both the family and the business. It also involves developing and nurturing the talent of the next generation of managers, making hard choices about the business and the family, facing up to conflict and resolving it, and letting go so the next generation of managers and owners can stretch their wings and take the company and the family to new levels.

The 10 most common and costly mistakes appear below with some discussion of each. As you read the mistakes, pay special attention to which of the 10 are family mistakes and which are technical mistakes. It cannot be overstated - the key to estate planning and business succession is *communication* among the family, management, and other stakeholders.

Mistake One - The Big Four

The following four mistakes are so pervasive that they are grouped together in one category. In spite of hiring the finest attorneys, accountants, and financial planners, nine out of 10 family business owners have made at least one of these four mistakes!

The first of the big four mistakes is the failure to execute documents properly or in a timely manner. It is not uncommon to find family business owners who have high quality legal documents but who have failed to sign them because they have never made the time to go by the attorney's office to execute them. The best documents in the world are valueless unless the client has them properly executed. It is critical that someone on the team follows through to make sure the documentation "punch list" is complete.

The second of the big four mistakes is outdated wills and other documents. Estate planning is not a destination; it is a journey. Family situations, business conditions, and tax laws change. If your wills or other legal documents have not been reviewed and revised within the past three years, chances are good they are not as family or tax smart as they should be. Family business owners are often shocked to find that an ex-spouse or ex-in-law is still mentioned as a beneficiary in their testamentary documents. Or they may find that a bank with whom they had severed relationships is still trustee and, as such, potentially has a tremendous amount of influence over the family's personal and professional lives in the future. Outdated documents can cost tremendous sums of money or create tremendous emotional toll on the family.

The third of the big four is the failure to properly title assets. This simple mistake could cost heirs up to $250,000! Both spouses should have assets worth at least $1.5 million titled solely in their names to be certain they will be able to fully utilize the unified transfer credit exemption for estate taxes. Be advised, jointly titled assets may not work! Why take the chance on creating unnecessary taxation when there is a foolproof method for handling this oversight?

The fourth of the big four - and the one that is generally most costly to family business estates - is the incorrect ownership of life insurance. The common assumption is that life insurance proceeds are tax free. That is true when it comes to income taxes, but life insurance proceeds are estate taxable. Most life insurance agents are so eager to get signatures on the bottom line that they don't take the time to ensure that the policy is properly owned. For example, a $1 million insurance policy could end up costing $500,000 in unnecessary, avoidable taxes if it's owned improperly. Most attorneys can draft an irrevocable life insurance trust for a reasonable sum of money that permanently and irrevocably prevents the government from taxing life insurance proceeds. Pay attention to corporate owned life insurance; it can be as big a problem as individual insurance and is generally not a good alternative method of insurance ownership.

Mistake Two - Planning In A Vacuum

Most family business owners have firm ideas about how to dispose of the business and how the estate should be divided. The standard procedure for handling estate planning for a successful family business owner is for planners to meet with Dad (and possibly Mom), find out how he wants to execute his documents, and to get the project done. However, in complicated business situations, the textbook legal and technical solutions to estate planning simply don't work. It is critical that everyone understands the family issues and the goals and objectives of the stakeholders before entering into complicated and sometimes irreversible estate plans.

Here is an example of why it is important to discuss everyone's desires before embarking on estate planning. The owner of a successful company had his attorney and CPA draw up an estate plan which left a part of his business to his daughter and another part to his son. Both of the children were employees in the company. Two other children who didn't work in the firm were to be given other assets. Only after confidential interviews did the FBO discover that the two employee children didn't feel capable of continuing the business after Dad's death. Furthermore, estate taxes were likely to wipe out the balance of the estate which was destined to go to the two non-employee children. Either they would inherit nothing, or the business would have to be divided among employee and non-employee siblings. Had Dad not found out what the rest of the family wanted, the outcome could have been devastating.

This family business owner's estate plan was doomed to fail because he had not bothered to find out what his children really wanted. He was amazed by what his children really thought about themselves, the family, and the business. Because of his hard work and sacrifice, the business was certainly the owner's to dispose of as he wished, but, like most successful FBOs, he was appalled to think that a lifetime of hard work would count for little or nothing after his demise.

FBOs create unintended consequences by not evaluating the concerns and desires of their heirs and incorporating those concerns into the business succession and estate plans. Children of strong FBOs are sometimes unwilling or unable to tell their parents their innermost feelings about the ultimate disposition of the family business or other assets. It often takes an objective third party to ask the right questions to solicit the true feelings of all stakeholders.

Mistake Three - Poor Communication

Closely related to planning in a vacuum is poor intergeneral communication and/or intragenerational communication. Family businesses often operate under the philosophy that "because we love each other, that's enough to get us through anything..." While it's true that family love is an abiding strength, it's simply not enough to get a family through difficult times of frustration and intergenenerational or intragenerational conflict. The lack of formal family and business procedures can render communications so poor that they cease altogether. While family members may love each other, they may not like each other very much as business partners.

Another communication issue in family companies is the confusion centered around conflict. Most family companies aren't clear about the difference between constructive resolution of conflict and the simple suppression of conflict. When children are small, Mom and Dad have the physical size and moral authority to simply suppress conflict. They can say, "go to your room," or "stop picking on your sister." At that life stage, the children have no choice but to comply. By the time the children are in their 30s or 40s, the parents may no longer have the physical size and moral authority with which they can suppress conflict. Even if they did, it's probably not the best course of action. In the absence of practical conflict resolution techniques, communication breaks down.

Another communication problem in family enterprises is the lack of a common vision. In second or subsequent generation companies, it's not unusual to find sibling partners or cousin consortiums in which individuals have radically different views of where the company could and should head. The Bible says a man cannot serve two masters, and that's true in a family enterprise where there's a lack of a common vision.

Mistake Four - Leaving the Business to Mom

In discussing mistake four, it is important to note that the following comments are not meant in any way to be sexist; this problem can apply to either gender. However, most family enterprises that have been successful over the last 15 years or more were started by and continue to be led by men. Therefore, for the purposes of brevity, we will use the old fashioned model of a father who runs the business and a mother who runs the family.

Most estate plans for family business owners leave the stock in the business either outright or in trust to Mom. This practice is standard with lawyers and financial planners who, virtually without fail, leave significant assets to the surviving spouse because of the unlimited marital deduction from estate taxes. Dad agrees to this approach because the family company is the best investment he ever made, and he thinks he is giving Mom security and an income stream after he is gone.

This is another example of family business owners planning their estates in a vacuum. No one bothers to ask Mom if she wants the business! If she is not a management employee in the company, she will be dependent on her children or non-family managers to run the company successfully. If they do not, they have jeopardized Mom's old age security. If, conversely, the business explodes in value because of the successful management of the subsequent generation, they have inflated Mom's estate to the point where the taxes could potentially be crippling. Leaving the company to Mom is a double edged sword.

In virtually 100% of family interviews, Mom states clearly and unequivocally that she wants to be financially independent and have long term financial security. She does not want the responsibility of running or owning the business. She doesn't want dependence on the business managers or her children. She doesn't want the potential for conflict between owners who are looking for stability and a regular income stream and managers who are looking to build the company and reinvest profits. She also doesn't want personal indemnification for the business debt!

This estate planning mistake can create major conflict within the family. It is rarely beneficial to Mom or the business for her to inherit the ownership as a simple tax avoidance measure. This is a perfect example of the tax tail wagging the dog.

Mistake Five - Nobody Knows What to Do When They Get Home from Your Funeral

Once the principal owner is gone and the shock of his passing has worn off, the question is invariably present: "What do we do now?" While no one wants to think of one's mortality, dying is a part of living. Because the nature of most FBOs is to be very private about their estate planning, the family usually knows little about the assets to be divided, little about how the company is to be owned and managed, and nothing about what Dad expects for the family after he is gone. This lack of information creates uncertainty and turmoil in the family as well as the business. It is important that your family hear directly from you, or at least have in writing from you, your wishes for how the family and the business are to be managed after your demise.

The son of a successful businessman, a great success in his own right, commented that his brother hadn't spoken to him in two years. His dad gave each of the brothers an opportunity to come into the family business, and only one of the siblings had decided to do so. When Dad died, he left the business to the employee son and assumed that everyone would feel that this was an equitable arrangement. Not so. The other son felt that he had been treated unfairly and blamed his brother for convincing Dad to give him a lesser amount of assets. He had an attorney propose that his brother pay him a seven figure settlement. The subsequent disagreement caused an irreparable split between the brothers.

The brother who inherited the company explained that he had nothing whatsoever to do with his father's estate plan. He wished that his father had brought the family together and explained to them all what was to be done when he died. He lamented the fact that, due to the unresolved conflict, he had been unable to spend Thanksgiving or Christmas together with his brother, and the rift did not appear to be going away. Simple planning and communication could have prevented a family split and untold heartache.

Mistake Six - No Exit Strategy

When men and women become accustomed to depending on their wits, judgment, and experience to build successful companies, they can develop "superman syndrome" and come to believe that there's nothing they can't handle. They feel invincible and think they will always have the energy and drive to continue to build their enterprises. They inadvertently build traps by not having exit strategies from their businesses.

The time to develop an escape strategy is when the owner is in his early to mid-50s. The primary question is whether to keep or sell the business. There are many factors which go into that decision, but the keep or sell decision is fundamental in planning an escape strategy.

By age 55, the keep or sell decision should be firmly made. If the decision is to keep the business, it is crucial that the FBO become a teacher to develop the successor leaders in his company. If the best solution is to sell the company, there is time to prepare it, to market it, and to conclude a transaction.

Consider the consequences for not developing an exit strategy. A 70 year old businessman was distraught. He spent his entire adult life in the business and had enjoyed building it. He was approached in his 60s about developing an exit strategy, but he scoffed at the thought and couldn't find the time because of the hectic pace that managing his company demanded. Now, he was desperate. His key employees were approximately his age and they weren't likely candidates to succeed him (not to mention their lack of capital). He had engaged business brokers, but none were able to find a buyer at a price remotely approaching what the owner felt it was worth. As his energy and drive faded, he feared that he would have to sell the company for the value of the equipment. At fire sale prices, the vultures would get a bargain, and the FBO's old age security would be compromised. Because he waited too long to develop an exit strategy, he robbed himself of the real value of his business and created fear and uncertainty for his old age.

Mistake Seven - Failure to Recognize And Plan For Transition

Transition is a process in and of itself. The ideal transition process allows for about 10 years for the gradual exit of the senior generation in favor of junior generation management. Succession plans that are shorter in duration than about 10 years seriously erode the chances of business success over time. Senior generation members have many reasons why they are uncomfortable letting go (some of which have been detailed in previous chapters); among them are concerns about:

• how next generation family members will get along
• lack of leadership

- lack of work hours and commitment
- lack of adaptation to technological change
- lack of financial security
- disappointing some children if others are named to positions of higher responsibility
- surviving spouse's financial security

Junior generation family members have their own list of concerns:

- following in the footsteps of a highly successful parent
- getting along with siblings or cousins
- lack of accountability among family members who don't pull their weight
- fear of inequitable stock distributions between employee and non-employee siblings
- fear of senior generation reentering the business and reasserting control
- fear of estate taxation
- lack of confidence in the business and individual capabilities necessary for success

The only way to answer the concerns of both senior and junior generations in the transition planning process is to start early and to approach it strategically. Figure One below outlines what typical family business succession looks like. The senior generation wakes up one day at age 65 or 70 and realizes that after 30 or more years of hard work he's tired and, in spite of his financial success, hasn't really led much of a life outside the business. He then looks to his junior generation children or managers and says, "you know what? I'm tired and would like to do a little bit of living before my time is up. Therefore, I'm retiring at the end of this year and you'll be taking over the family business." The transition event has been thrust upon the next generation managers without adequate time and preparation. Both generations overestimate the depth of the succeeding generation's skills, abilities, and knowledge. They simply can't make up the absence of the additional 20 or 30 years of experience accumulated by the senior generation. The junior generation, which has been kept on the sidelines for many years, is now expected to make a quantum leap in their talents, knowledge, skills, and abilities and become capable of running the business as well as or better than the senior generation.

Figure 1

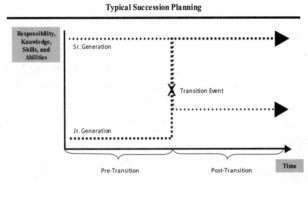

Figure 2

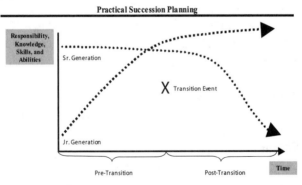

A more practical and successful planning methodology is outlined in Figure Two. In Figure Two, the senior generation has decided that he'd like to leave the business in seven to 10 years. At that decision point, he begins a grooming, teaching, and mentoring process so that the junior generation will possess the tools and skills they'll need to run the business successfully well before the senior generation decides to step away. This allows for both generations to be comfortable and armed with the knowledge they'll need to be successful in the post-transition world. Unfortunately, the practical succession planning outlined in Figure Two is all too rare.

Mistake Eight - Giving (Or Selling) Family Business Stock To Your Children Equally

Parents have a strong desire to treat their children fairly and equally. This desire is consistent throughout a parent's life. If, when the kids were small, one got a Hershey bar in her Christmas stocking, all the kids got Hershey bars in their stockings. If one child got a bicycle at age seven, all the children got a bicycle at age seven. When it comes time to divide the greatest Christmas gift of all, most parents fall back on lifetimes of training and reflexively decide to divide the family business pie into equal slices.

Most business families have employee and non-employee children. The potential for conflict between employee and non-employee owners in a family company is tremendous. Often, their goals and objectives for the family business are diametrically opposed. Non-employee owners want a reasonable current return on their investment and the ability to have input into corporate policy. Employee shareholders want growth, reinvestment of the lion's share of the profits, and a free hand to run the business as they see fit. The conflicting demands on corporate resources are often too much for families and businesses to bear.

In addition, there are fairness issues. What does a non-employee owner actually have in terms of an inheritance? Shares of stock might look nice when valued for financial statement purposes, but the reality for most family companies is that those shares are as valueless as the paper they are printed on. Moms and Dads rely on conditioned responses to treat their children equally when it comes to dividing the family business, but that logic is flawed.

A father built a successful company. When he died, he divided his business pie equally between his son and daughter. His son was the president of the company and worked 60 or more hours per week to discharge his management responsibilities. The sister was married to a college professor and lived in a nearby state. The family company was very profitable, and the annual S distributions were well over $200,000 per year. While this situation was not perfect for the employee son, it was tolerable.

After a few years of this arrangement, the corporation needed to make a significant capital investment to update equipment. The bank was happy to lend $5 million to the corporation provided it could secure a resolution signed by the corporate directors. The employee brother called his non-employee sister; her first question was, "What will this transaction do to my S distributions?" The answer was clear; most of the company's profits would have to be used for debt service, and S distributions would have to be severely restricted for the foreseeable future. The sister refused to sign the resolution!

The brother was left with two choices. Either he could borrow the money and solely provide a personal guarantee that the money would be repaid, or he could dispense with his plans to update the company's equipment. Neither choice was very palatable. The personal guarantee on the loan would mean that he was taking all of the risk for this transaction with the possibility of only 50% of the reward. If he failed to reinvest in his business, the future profitability of the company was constrained. To say the least, relations between the brother and sister were severely strained and possibly damaged to the point where they could not be repaired.

Wouldn't the children have been better served if Dad had put appropriate assets in the hands of the employee child and other appropriate assets in the hands of the non-employee child? Wouldn't the potential for conflict between these two siblings with differing personal and business objectives be reduced to a manageable level? Most family business commentators stress that employee children should inherit stock in the enterprises where they work, and non-employee children should be *equitably* treated with other assets, preferably outside the scope of the business.

The problem becomes more complex when there are multiple employee children. If an FBO accepts the premise that he'll only give stock in the enterprise to employee children, how does he go about treating the employee children equitably when they have different positions, abilities, and potentials for leading? For example, is it fair for the future CEO child to inherit the same amount of stock as a child who works on the loading dock and expresses no interest in the management or direction of the company? How is it fair that the child on the loading dock has an equal voice in corporate affairs? A business generally won't run as well with ownership divided equally among employee and non-employee children as it would if one of the children clearly had the role of quarterback. There are notable exceptions to this rule, and your family may be a perfect example of why rules are made to be broken; however, it is generally true that a successful team needs to have one - and only one - quarterback in order to maximize its success and avoid the conflict common when there are too many players in the huddle.

Mistake Nine - Holding On Too Long

This book, as well as countless others, advocates for senior generation family members to gradually release the reins of control over time, yet this continues to be a tremendous issue in many family companies. As we saw in Chapter Two, there are many psychological as well as practical reasons why successful entrepreneurs are reluctant to let go of the businesses they began. The message that cannot be stated too strongly is that in holding on too long, senior generation family members inadvertently damage the things they love the most: the business, their children, and perhaps even the grandchildren. There are business, family, tax, and other rationales for letting go. While there's an exception to every rule, it can't be stated too strongly that holding on too long with an irrational desire to control the affairs of the business and your children is a dire mistake. It's simply good stewardship to perpetuate your business and pass opportunity along to your children and to key non-family managers.

Mistake Ten - Giving Too Much Too Soon

When FBOs are asked why they work so hard to build successful companies and accumulate wealth, they typically respond by saying they did it for their families. While it is understood that they don't owe their children anything, it is only natural they would want to share the wealth they have created with those they love.

Many FBOs devoted long hours and tremendous energy to their companies to get them off the ground. They were gone on business trips during various parts of the year, and they worked nights and weekends to make their dreams come true. When the children were young, the FBO was often absent, and it was Mom's responsibility to handle every aspect of the family's daily living. Later in life, when FBOs have climbed the ladder of success, they try to make up for the time when they were absent from the children's early years by lavishing expensive gifts, cash, or vacations on them.

There are significant problems with giving children too much too soon. All parents want their children to become productive members of society who know what it's like to have to work and make their own way in the world. While there are problems with not sharing any of your wealth with your children, the greater threat is to overdo it and shower them with too much.

There is a real need to balance the necessity of strategic gifts with the mandate of not spoiling your children. It isn't an easy balance to strike, but it is achievable. Vehicles like the Family Incentive Trust™, limited liability companies, and other techniques make it possible for you to move assets from your generation to theirs without doing unintentional harm to your children by providing a lifestyle that they do not earn. The best advice is to not allow your children to become

85

dependent on you for handouts to support a lifestyle they can't sustain on their own. This is a case where the tax savings tail should not wag the dog. Doing what is best from an estate planning point of view may not coincide with doing what is best from a family point of view.

Conclusion

This discussion of the 10 most common and costly estate planning mistakes made by family business owners has been long on problems and short on solutions. This is by design. As doctors say, prescription before diagnosis is malpractice. Each family business is unique in its own way, and your advisors must guide you on which business succession, family planning and estate planning techniques make the most sense in your situation.

It is critically important to avoid the 10 most common and costly mistakes, and there are fairly straightforward techniques available to avoid slip-ups. A thread that runs throughout family firms is the sense of stewardship the owners have for their families and businesses. It is this sense of stewardship that mandates that family business owners engage the very best advisors available to avoid problems and maximize opportunities whenever possible. The family business is the best vehicle ever invented (other than religion) to promote and transfer family values, and smart planning can help your company - and your values - survive for generations to come.

CHAPTER SIX

IMPROVING BUSINESS FAMILY
COMMUNICATIONS

PRESCRIPTION: Your business family must develop an organized, formal, and regularly scheduled mechanism for improving and sustaining sound communications.

Many, if not most, business family problems begin with poor and infrequent communication. How many business crises could have been averted over the years if the families had simply taken a few hours a month to have a meeting so that everyone's views, opinions, and goals could be aired openly in a non-judgmental setting? Families assume that because they love each other that affection alone can make up for a host of other personal or business shortcomings. That may be true in the short run, but over time a lack of effective communication can sabotage even the most loving business family. A troubled family will lead ultimately to a troubled family business.

There are many family injuries, some of which are so minor as to be forgotten by other family members, which can come home to roost in the family company. Unlike physical injuries which are easily observed, family or emotional injuries are not easily observable until they reach critical mass and result in a blowup. Among the items contributing to trauma to the family system are parental neglect, favoritism (or the perception of favoritism), the quest to earn Dad's blessing, and sibling rivalry. Simply discussing these family issues and bringing them into the light of day can lead to a remarkable turnaround in business family cooperation and productivity.

Everyone has heard the old saying that an ounce of prevention is worth a pound of cure. When it comes to family businesses, this cliché is uncannily accurate. In prescribing cures for family businesses, it is helpful to think of the example that public health uses when identifying types of disease prevention. Primary prevention refers to the prevention of a disease *before* it occurs. Family businesses experience common challenges that are easily anticipated, and primary prevention techniques are fairly simple and easy to execute. Secondary prevention refers to early identification of the problem and proactive intervention. The interventions can address the issues at hand to help resolve individual or group problems which contribute to family trauma. Tertiary prevention refers to treatment of a disorder *after* it's full blown and attempts to prevent greater problems in the future. When a family conflict has already caused serious problems in the business or the family, it is still possible to help them look at their constructive options for getting on a more positive path, selling the company, or getting a "business divorce."

In this chapter, we will examine ways to improve family communications to promote understanding, harmony, and fairness. In cases where family communication has taken a turn for the worse, we will look at ways to restore healthy, balanced interaction.

Why Is Family Business Communication So Difficult?

Some families will stop at nothing to avoid discussion of controversial issues. They fear that a controversial issue will raise not just the issue itself but the family's history of hurts, disappointments, assumptions, unrealized expectations, etc. Every family conversation runs the risk of resurrecting uncomfortable moments in the history of the business or the family. The baggage inherent in family relationships gets in the way of open and straight-forward communication. Many families have the mistaken idea that the measure of a successful or healthy family is a lack of conflict; that's not true. It is a family's method of reacting to conflict that's the true measure of health and emotional maturity.

Having a family meeting can be a nerve racking and risky event. Someone could cry, tempers might flair, someone may storm out of the room, or somebody may be confronted with uncomfortable realities or perceptions. However, the risk of conducting a constructive meeting with your family is far less than the risk inherent in *not talking*. Talking things out can help the business and the family resolve a host of issues. Old hurts and misunderstandings can be put away forever. Old family assumptions and traditions that have outlived their usefulness can be put away too. Everyone has a voice in determining a positive outcome for the entire family. The family learns new methods of deliberation and decision-making. Everyone in the group has an opportunity to "buy in." Everyone can, perhaps for the first time, become a stakeholder in both the business and the family. The possibility for a win-win situation is vastly increased when there is positive communication. The future for the family and the business can become clearer, less threatening, and more energizing for all involved.

Families are biological entities with all the associated imperfections. Businesses are like machines where biological - that is to say human - behavior gets in the way of business outputs and results. For most families in business together, family beliefs get transferred into the business machine. Some examples of common family myths that become part of the business are:

- The family agrees unanimously before making any decision and moving forward.
- All family members are eligible for jobs in the family business.
- Every family employee is treated equally with respect to pay.
- Leaving the employment of the business is the same as disassociating from the family.
- The business is a part of our family and must never be sold.
- That's the way we've always done it here, and, because we have been so successful and profitable, we don't need to change with the times.
- This business is no place for women.
- The business can support the lifestyles of everyone in the family in a first class manner.

Emerson said, "a foolish consistency is the hobgoblin of small minds." A foolish consistency, when it comes to destructive or obsolete family rules, can be foolish and devastating for the family enterprise!

Family business researchers have identified at least four types of tensions that must be anticipated and overcome to have a successful family business transition:

- Tension within the founder of the business having to do with the realization of his quests for heroic stature and heroic mission.
- Tension between generations.
- Tension within succeeding generations (i.e. between brothers

and sisters as they compete for the title of first among equals).
• Tension between the leader of the family business and long-term suppliers, employees, and customers.

The first tension that founders struggle with has to do with the twin pillars of heroic stature and heroic mission. These tensions make it difficult for successful entrepreneurs to confront their eventual loss of capacity and ultimate exit from the company. Their personal identities become so intertwined with those of the company that they fear the day when they are no longer CEO as the time when they will no longer have a personal identity. They also fear that if they are not present to steer the company ship it will flounder on the rocks. There is a role confusion, and the entrepreneur confuses his roles of boss at work and father at home. Entrepreneurs often feel trapped, and there is no escape hatch with which to get out.

The second group of tensions, those between the generations, may create irrational fear in the parents that their children are abandoning them and leaving them to die. Psychologists have observed that there is a destructive oedipal competition for the business between fathers and sons as they struggle to determine which male has the primary relationship within the firm. When the discussions of succession come at a time when both fathers and sons are in turbulent life stages, animosity and hostility are far more likely (see Chapter Three).

The third set of tensions has do with sibling rivalry or jealously among cousins. Selection of a successor and charges of favoritism can cause problems as the chosen one attempts to assert his will over those not chosen (and vice versa).

The fourth set of tensions relates to challenges outside of the family. Long term employees are a particular source of tension as the new generation of business leaders begins to assert its will over the direction of the company. The former leader's lieutenants may grieve over their lost relationships which kept them close to the seat of power. Successors may be viewed as intruders who lack experience and are still "wet behind the ears."

What are families to do about these four common types of intrigues? Here are four simple tools to help:

- Anticipating these four tensions is the key! The tasks of the outgoing leader should begin with planning a strategic exit which includes a smooth passing of the baton to the next generation of leaders.
- Preparing the overall company for the coming leadership transition.
- Advising all stakeholders of the coming changes and facilitating constructive discussion among them.
- Finding a new heroic mission for the withdrawing leader and a new source of heroic stature so that he doesn't leave his identity behind him when he walks out the door for the final time. He must be aware that his success is symbolized by the company he is leaving, but is not limited only to past achievements. There can be many new and exciting achievements in the future if the departing leader will only open his mind and heart to them.

Entrepreneurs who are undergoing exits from their companies face overwhelming loneliness. Having a network of outside contacts, perhaps peers who have been through similar experiences, is particularly valuable. Most strong entrepreneurs are not likely to request help because it may make them appear weak. However, the counsel of experienced friends, peers, or consultants can help departing leaders pass the baton successfully and create a new reason for waking up every morning.

What Are The Usual Sources Of Family Conflict?

Most business families think that their conflicts, mild or bitter, are unique to them. However, the reality is that most families stumble over the same hurdles, and the solutions that work for one family may, in fact, prove to work just as well for other families in business together. The following is a short discussion of some of the sources of family dissension.

Violation of family members' senses of fair play. It is a common assumption in most families that all children will be treated equally, and parents have always worked desperately to be even-handed with their children to avoid even the appearance of favoritism. However, when it comes to the family enterprise, treating the children equally becomes impossible due to their different talents, strengths, ambitions, and life stages.

Take an example of a family with three children. As the CEO of the family company, the oldest child has lifted sales from $10 million per year at the beginning of his leadership to $30 million just 10 short years later. Profits have risen at the same rate. The middle child chose a career in the ministry and lives out of state. The third child became involved in drugs and alcohol at an early age, has been in rehab several times, and has worked in a series of menial jobs with frequent handouts from Mom and Dad to keep afloat financially. If this fictitious Mom and Dad were to treat each of the children equally, circumstances would dictate that they give the family enterprise to the children in one-third increments. This couldn't be more unfair to the successful oldest child who has built the company from a relatively modest enterprise into a profit making powerhouse. It is also not fair to the non-employee siblings who would have little to no voice in day-to-day management of the company and would lack the ability to genuinely influence corporate decision-making. If the two non-CEO children did decide to band together and pool their strength to form a two-thirds block of voting power, they could force their sibling CEO to bend to their wishes. But what would be the result for their family relationship, and what would be the likelihood of this business family enjoying each other's company over the holidays?

Just because it doesn't make business sense to divide this pie equally among the three children, that doesn't mean that the ultimate division should be left an open question. The point is that in order to avoid violating senses of fair play or justice in the family, outcomes must be discussed ahead of time to make sure everyone is fully informed. Without a fair dissemination of information, it is virtually assured there will be hurt feelings and unrealized expectations which could lead to serious family breakdown.

Feeling unacknowledged by other members of the family. Family members often feel that their talents, strengths, potentials, or contributions are ignored by others, especially their parents. Parents, especially those of the World War II generation or older, are not generally full of praise and positive affirmations. They were raised in an atmosphere where success was expected, and they didn't need to be praised. The only kind of feedback they exhibited was criticism or corrective action. Children in family businesses begun by this generation may feel they are not valued for their contributions or they are not affirmed as responsible adults.

Feelings of powerlessness. Some family business leaders are extremely autocratic in their management styles. The entrepreneurial habits which made them successful may have also made them weak in terms of sharing responsibility and listening to others. Many family business children feel powerless because their fathers - even at age 70 and beyond - refuse to give up any management responsibilities and continue to hold on to 100% of the stock. The children fear that they will never get a chance to stretch their wings, have their days in the sun, or that they will be at retirement age themselves by the time they get their chance to steer the company ship.

Role confusion between the business and the family. Family business fathers often rule their businesses with an iron hand. Sometimes they bring those iron hands home and try to rule the family in the same way. However, anyone who has tried to reason with an over-tired three year old who is determined to have her own way knows that, no matter how much of a colossus in the business world you might be, your will is nothing when matched against that of a crying, thrashing three year old.

Family issues are most appropriately handled in a non-judgmental, nurturing, accepting, caring, and loving way. Business issues are handled dispassionately, with an eye to the bottom line, rationally, and in the best interest of the company whose goal is to maximize profits. It is easy to see that people in family businesses migrate from the business dynamic to the family dynamic without serious consideration of which role one should be playing. For example, how should a family business mother approach a situation where she will have to fire one of her employee children? Textbooks say that she should wear the hat of the business manager and approach the meeting in a dispassionate and rational way. What mother could truly be dispassionate about the potential trauma of letting her child go?

There are several common myths about family business communication and conflict that cause family members to throw up their hands and to settle into apathy and reactive behavior. However, most family business difficulties are resolvable and can be worked out to produce win-win results for all involved. These myths are just that - myths. They must be identified and eliminated so the family can move on to positive solutions and improved communications.

Three Common Family Business Communication Myths

The first common myth is that families do not have conflict if those involved really love each other. The opposite is closer to reality. We don't have conflict with people we do not care about. Only those whose opinions and views we value have the abilities to put us on the defensive and cause conflict. If conflict isn't addressed proactively and creatively, tensions simmer just below the surface and can explode with the tiniest of sparks. Conflict is a fact of life in families and in business, and it must be resolved.

The second myth is that since Mom or Dad (or brother or sister or anyone else) won't change, there is nothing I can do about the situation. This myth is incorrect also; it allows another party to have control over you and on your ability to shape your destiny. You, at the very least, can become more self aware and work on positive changes and on modeling effective behavior. Conflict resolution, no matter how frustrating your situation may be, begins with you. There are things you can do to create a positive, nurturing climate for other parties to find their own ways towards solutions.

The third myth about family business communication has its roots in the things we assume. For example, a family member may be frustrated at what he perceives as the lack of progress in succession planning and leadership development. He raised the issue with Dad five years ago, and Dad reacted negatively. Therefore, the son assumes that same five-year-old negative reaction is the answer to his concern now and forever. He is not being fair to Dad in making an assumption. Dad may have had several experiences which have radically changed his thinking on the subject over the last five years, but he is waiting for his son to show a spark of interest and enthusiasm for pursuing change. Dad *assumes* that the son will come to him when the planets align and he feels that he is ready for the top job. Both parties are making incorrect assumptions that are holding back the family and the business from moving forward.

Triangling is one of the most common barriers to effective family and business communications. Triangling is a term therapists use to describe a situation where two people, for whatever reason, have difficulty communicating directly, and so they coerce a third party to be their "shuttle communicator."

A Communication Triangle

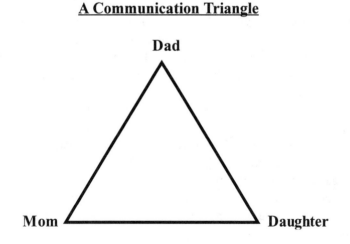

Dad

Mom   **Daughter**

In the example above, a family business daughter is uncomfortable communicating her frustration at her lack of promotion to her father, so she enlists her mom to apply pressure on Dad on her behalf. Mom goes to Dad to intervene, and Dad responds negatively by saying that Mom doesn't know a thing about business and should keep her nose out of it. Now, instead of having one family member who is in distress, there are three. This is an example of a triangle which did not produce the intended result.

A triangle becomes a problem when bringing in the third person becomes a habit that keeps the original pair from settling their differences with each other. Triangling is a common way people deal with anxiety; they adjust their behavior so they will feel more comfortable and, therefore, less anxious. When we feel anxiety, we want to move away from the situation that creates the anxiety. Triangling temporarily decreases tension between people, but it does not solve the original problems that created the situation. It acts like a valve on a pressure cooker which allows pressure to bleed off while continuing the cooking process.

When anxiety begins to increase between two individuals one or both move away from the situation. That movement can be either toward another person (like the mother in the example above) or toward an object, task, or vice such as working more hours or consuming more alcohol.

Triangle patterns tend to repeat themselves. Once a particular triangle has worked a time or two it becomes patterned in the people involved and becomes relatively inflexible over time. Every time one person experiences anxiety, the individual tends to seek the same person or thing to help decrease the tension; the behavior becomes a habit. For the person who is drawn into the triangle, the process also becomes automatic. That person wants to help, and providing a shoulder to cry on makes both participants feel better.

Mom is the most commonly involved third party in triangles because of her position as CEO - Chief Emotional Officer. Mom wants harmony in the family and the business. She often acts as the buffer between rugged fathers who are gruff and uncomfortable showing their emotions and children who feel they are unfairly victimized by Dad's desire for control. It is a perfectly natural response for Mom to want to patch things up whenever she feels that her husband and children are not enjoying a given level of harmony.

Triangles don't have to be destructive in family companies. They can provide temporary relief when tensions are high, but they are not useful in solving the underlying human or business issues that led to the rise of anxiety in the first place. Only direct communication between the two parties experiencing the tension and constructive, win-win resolutions to their real or imagined differences will pave the way for harmonious communications. Triangling is an escape, a release valve, and feels good in the short term. However, in family businesses where communication is critical in order to preserve harmony, triangling can become a destructive mechanism which prevents legitimate discussion, handling, and resolution of problems.

Family Systems Theory

Dr. Murray Bowen developed Family Systems Theory when he worked at the Menninger Clinic and later when he moved to the National Institute of Mental Health. His approach is based on the theory that we repeat what we came out of and that we are who we are because of our family systems. Each generation in the family repeats the patterns of the preceding generations; we evolved as unwittingly as our parents did before us and their parents before them. The family systems theory sees what is going on in the individual as inseparable from the broader family network of relationships in which the individual is embedded. As an example, Dr. Bowen found that when treated on an individual basis, schizophrenics could make progress. However, when the patient returned to the family of origin, the schizophrenic behavior recurred. He came to believe that something occurs in the schizophrenic's family that related to or precipitated the schizophrenic behavior. His theory states that only when families are viewed as a system - not as a set of individual people -

can problems be understood and changes successfully made. Dr. Bowen's theory can be summarized in a few critical points:

- The family is a system.
- Systems have rules, messages, patterns, or expectations for behavior.
- We can and do learn behaviors different from those of our families of origin.
- When stress arises, we revert to the pattern of our original family systems unless we learn to short circuit that reversion and apply newly learned behaviors.
- Every family member becomes aware of his dependence on others in the system and a wide range of "alliances" for helping or hurting other members in the family.

Dr. Bowen's theories have helped an entire generation of family business consultants get beyond looking at one or two individuals in a family intervention to take a broader perspective of the entire family as the client or patient.

Tools for Improving Family Business Communication

Family business communication is conducted informally virtually all of the time. The desire to keep harmony in the family causes most families to go to desperate lengths to avoid discussing controversial or potentially hurtful issues. Upon examination, this reasoning is rather ridiculous. Avoiding controversial issues doesn't make them go away; it simply means that family members engage in wishful thinking and hope the stress issues will disappear. For family business owners, who are the most pragmatic and commonsensical people in the world, this is indeed curious and counterintuitive behavior. They meet other challenges head on, but family business communication challenges are avoided like the plague!

Families must work to formalize their communication skills for the mutual good. Relationships are the key to family business success, and sound relationships don't happen by themselves. Most businesses can survive the threats of competition, economic ups and downs, and changes in technology, but the deterioration of interpersonal relationships can devastate the business and tear the family apart. Factors that have impact on the family are likely to have impact on the business and vice versa. Families are rarely taught how to build good relationships, but there are skills that can be learned to make working together and living together more rewarding and enjoyable.

The foundation for building good relationships is *open and honest communication*. A little work in this area can pave the way for significantly improved relationships. Family members must be willing to address issues that are touchy or controversial. Active listening is a vital part of good communication. Covey advises that it is important to seek to understand rather than to be understood. Like a building constructed on a faulty foundation, relationships that do not start with honest and open communications are doomed to crumble.

Common values are important to a family. Values like honesty, trustworthiness, stewardship, loyalty, hard work, harmony, tolerance, and courtesy are common qualities that most families seek. It is important that business families have agreements on the values that are vitally important to their respective families.

Shared visions are another important factor. Families in business with each other rarely talk about shared vision, but building meaningful and caring relationships requires agreement on the outcomes all parties would like to see.

Agreeing on *expectations* is also vital. For example, if the first two generations of the family enterprise have the expectation that everyone will be punctual, and a member of the third generation is always fifteen to thirty minutes late for business and family functions, the latter is not meeting the expectations of his family. It is important that the family voice the expectations; the third generation family member may not even be aware that his lateness is viewed with disdain. It is not fair to other members of your family to have expectations which you are unwilling to communicate to them; how can they hit a target they can't even see?

Accountability is a building block in sound family relationships. There must be accountability for actions within the family just as there is accountability for responsibilities within the business.

Attitude is important. Do you demonstrate concern and care for your other family members, or do you demonstrate a disregard for their feelings and interests? Your attitude goes a long way toward establishing mutually fulfilling or broken relationships. Attitude is often demonstrated through body language and eye contact to a larger degree than the spoken word. Genuine attention and interest in other members of your family will encourage them to demonstrate the same to you.

Strong families are based on *contact* with each other. Spending time together helps strengthen family bonds, especially when that time is outside of the office. It is generally smart to avoid discussing business during family and social settings. Playing together can be as important as working together, and social interaction can help family members understand each other, learn about interests away from work, and develop a more balanced picture of other parties.

Understanding the family's *decision-making processes* can improve relationships. In previous generations, one strong leader made all the decisions at home and at work. When today's family members enter the family company, they're less likely to automatically accept these dictates, and that can cause intergenerational strain. Business families need to understand what authority will be shared at work as well as at home. As one family business patriarch stated, "we don't have time to turn this business into a democracy and take a vote on every decision." This is precisely why everyone needs to understand the process for making decisions, who can make them, and when they can be expected to be involved in the process. Stakeholders who feel they have input into their organizations will feel better about the relationships with other members of the business family when their views are solicited and valued.

Conflict resolution is important. Any family that denies it has conflict is in serious denial mode or either family members are simply afraid to disagree with each other. Either alternative can point to serious relational problems in the future. How does your family resolve conflict? Do you pretend that it doesn't exist, or do you get together with the appropriate person and discuss it? If the disagreement persists, do you call in an independent third party to help construct a resolution? Written understandings of the conflict resolution process *before conflict arises* will help prevent misunderstandings and hurt feelings when conflict does occur. Family meetings can be held on the subject of how to resolve conflicts when they do arise.

Mutual respect is essential in business families. The best way to get respect is to conduct yourself in a consistent and honorable way. You must treat others as persons of worth. Do you communicate honestly and openly? Are you accountable for your actions? Do you demonstrate as well as verbally embrace the values that are respected by others? If you talk down to others or treat them in a disrespectful way, don't be surprised when they give you the same treatment in return. When mutual respect is present in a relationship, a sound basis is established for ironing out any differences.

Finally, *trust* is the most important agreement in solid family relationships. Trust is something earned over time. Trust can also easily be lost through mistreatment of others, dishonest communication, conflict, and other intentional and unintentional actions. Once a trust relationship is broken, it is difficult to rebuild. Great care must be taken to be trustworthy at all times.

No family is perfect; all business families must work constantly to build goodwill and improved relationships. Families that work together and live together are mutually dependent on the family and the business. Sound relationships will cement the successes of both.

Conclusion

Family businesses are not the soap operas that television shows or newspapers make them out to be; however, some loving, well-intentioned families get at cross purposes with each other and "get stuck." This chapter has many useful suggestions for getting your business family "unstuck." One of the most important recommendations outlined above is when the family seems truly deadlocked over family or business issues, it is extremely valuable to bring in an objective advisor who can view the situation with no emotional baggage and help deliver constructive, positive solutions that create win-win feelings for all involved. The ability to view events with distance and clarity can help the business family move forward to regain the glory and gratification that is unique to a family company.

CHAPTER SEVEN

A TWELVE STEP EXIT STRATEGY FOR FAMILY BUSINESS OWNERS

PRESCRIPTION: Because your departure from your business is inevitable, plan and write out a specific program for your exit and the ascension of the next generation of leaders in your business.

> John Medlin, former Chairman of Wachovia Bank, upon his retirement: "In one day I went from *Who's Who* to who's he!"

For family business owners, their personal identities are intertwined with their business identities. "Retirement" for family business owners is a dirty word and can represent a time of personal crisis, a leap into a scary void which they are neither ready nor willing to face. As a historical example, Winston Churchill was re-elected as Prime Minister of Great Britain in 1951. He was 77 years old, deaf, and had had two strokes. He promised his cabinet that he would stay in office for only one year and then he would pass control to a younger man. When the time came, he broke his promise and muddled on in the Prime Minister position for four and a half more years, even enduring another stroke during that period. He simply could not see himself as anything but a man of heroic stature who wasn't ready to give up his access to power and influence.

Churchill's struggle at the end of his professional life is paralleled often in the world of sports. Who could ever forget Muhammad Ali coming back from several retirements only to be beaten unmercifully by younger, stronger men? Bjorn Borg suffered the same fate in tennis. Steve Young of the San Francisco 49ers became so addicted to fame and competition that he found it difficult to retire even after a series of concussions had put him at risk for permanent brain damage. The list goes on and on. Family business owners are like these famous people in a number of ways, not the least of which is their inability to walk away from their success while at their peaks.

Here is a recommendation for family business owners: *forget about retirement*. Retirement is a dirty word. FBOs see nothing exciting about retirement and fear that retirement equals death. They've seen their peers or social acquaintances go from being active, vital businessmen to retired old busybodies where they become bored, sedentary, and even unhealthy in short order. There is loss associated with retirement: loss of power, loss of attention, perceived loss of life's work, and potential loss of the heroic mission.

As the visionaries and leaders of their businesses, FBOs are identified with their organizations. Their departures from their companies can mean much more than their own personal retirements; it means that the critical success factors for their companies are in flux and changing.

Question: At what moment does a pilot begin landing an airplane? *Answer*: The moment after it becomes airborne. From the moment of takeoff, the pilot is focused on one goal. Even as his craft is gaining altitude, increasing speed, and making directional corrections, the pilot has one thought in mind - the safe landing of his aircraft and his passengers at the desired destination.

Question: When should a family business owner begin exiting his or her business? *Answer*: The moment after starting or assuming control of the company. Owners of family firms should always be focused on the goal of exiting their companies at a predetermined time with harmony in their families and the future success of the business assured. Stephen Covey in his classic book, *The Seven Habits of Highly Effective People*, reinforces the point with his second habit: **begin with the end in mind**. To a family business owner this means the first step must be to have a formal plan. Just as a pilot has to file a written flight plan before taking off, so should the owner of a closely held company have a written plan for how and when to exit his business. In *Alice In Wonderland*, the Cheshire Cat told Alice, "if you don't know where you are going, any road will take you there." Translated for family businesses this means: how will you know when you can and should exit if you don't have a plan?

The accounting firm Deloitte & Touche LLP conducted a survey which indicated that only 28% of closely held businesses have written succession plans. Empirical observation indicates that this figure is far lower. Why don't family business owners develop exit and succession plans? The most common answer is that they simply don't know how to. They are wonderful at selling cars, constructing buildings, or developing real estate, but they don't truly know how to develop formal business plans. Another reason is that they hate the thought of giving up control. The business is their biggest achievement; it is who they are. In some instances, they have not identified a successor because they fear that choosing one of their children over the others will lead to disharmony or dissension. Some family business owners are dependent on the company for their financial security in retirement, and they are unwilling to let go of the reins of power because they fear it may jeopardize their old age security.

However, all of these are excuses for not building a plan. To use the airplane analogy, if the pilot got sick or died in mid-flight, who would take over and ensure the safety of the passengers (the family) and the plane itself (the business)? While one cannot foresee the future, a wise man understands the value of guarding against unforeseen situations and planning for certain eventualities. Sooner or later every pilot must look for a place to land safely, and so must a leader of a family business. History will judge the current leader by how well he prepared his family and business for that safe landing.

For family business owners, the exit period is a stressful - if not crisis filled - time. When surveyed, the top 10 stressors of family business owners were:

1. Death of spouse
2. Divorce
3. Marital separation
4. Jail
5. Death of a close family member
6. Personal injury or illness
7. Marriage
8. Being fired
9. Marital reconciliation
10. Retirement

Top leaders are much less enthusiastic about the potential for retirement than hourly or middle management workers. Their skills aren't very easily transferred from one job to another. For example, a carpenter can easily take his skills from one home building company to another. The CEO of a $50 million petroleum distribution and convenience store operation ironically has much less opportunity when it comes to career alternatives. There are simply fewer job slots for CEOs than any other type of worker. Workers with the highest status, which included successful family business owners, are less willing to retire than those in lesser positions. Those with "Type A" personalities (aggressive, hard driving, impatient, and active) are less likely to retire than calmer types. It goes without saying that most family business owners are Type A personalities.

FBOs are not necessarily motivated by money or the desire to keep up with the Joneses. Rather, they have an internal need to create and to build their visions for their companies and families. For them work is much more than a job; it provides their personal identification, group belonging, and purpose in life. FBOs seek to have significant influence in shaping their communities and society at large. They live to work instead of working to live. They have an inner drive to excel and stand apart from others through the significance of their professional contributions. Simply put, they are driven to build their legacies.

In his book, *The Hero's Farewell*, Jeffrey Sonnenfeld found that the retirement of family business owners resembles the adjustment period of a terminally ill patient faced with the prospect of ultimate death. First, there is a period of denial. Second, there is a stage of anger. Third, there is a stage of bargaining. Fourth, there is a stage of depression. Fifth, the terminally ill patient arrives at the stage of acceptance. Family business owners who have reached the stage of acceptance have noted that two things helped provide them with the perspective needed to carry on in a successful "second career." The first is writing their memoirs, even if it is done for family, not publication, purposes. The second item is the importance of family, children, grandchildren, travel with spouses, and more time at home in general; these activities offer them rejuvenation and perspective. A retired chief executive said his first two years in retirement were the most difficult. After that initial period of adjustment, his second career was able to take on new meaning. The challenge, then, for family business owners is to build a new life while simultaneously avoiding post-retirement emptiness.

Sonnenfeld interviewed a group of 75 Young Presidents Organization members in the late 1980s to determine their attitudes toward retirement. Non-family heads of companies looked forward to retirement, felt that retirement should come no later than age 70, and cited attainment of their life's goals as their reason for retirement.

Founders of closely held companies said they *never* intended to retire, did not look forward to retirement, did not think age should limit their tenure, and would consider retirement only in cases of poor health, boredom, or because one of their children was ready to take over! Obviously, founders felt a much deeper emotional and psychological commitment to their companies than non-family presidents.

In the same survey, the founders of companies *never* thought of themselves as mentoring, coaching, counseling, advising, or teaching. When it came to their successors, they presented themselves as judges who would put candidates for leadership on trial assignments. When asked how they would like to be remembered after retirement, non-family members expressed goals such as the financial stability of the company, growth of the business, and market share as measuring sticks. Family managers' goals had to do with building deeper, more secure foundations for their companies, the company's overall success, and a marked concern for their employees. The difference between non-family managers' and family managers' responses are striking.

Departure Styles of Family Business CEOs

Sonnenfeld described four manners of exit for chief executives. He labeled the styles:

1. Monarchs
2. Generals
3. Ambassadors
4. Governors

Monarchs don't leave office until they're forced out through death or a management coup. Monarchs are the most attached to their roles as chief executives. Their stature and power are hard to let go. They emphasize profits less than the other types of leaders while putting greater emphasis on building the company (high sales and high asset growth). Monarchs typically ruled until death. They were consistently weak in choosing a successor, and, once chosen, they frequently undermined him.

Generals also must be forced to exit. They leave reluctantly, but plan to return. They can't wait to come out of retirement in order to rescue their companies from what they perceive as inept successors. Generals often develop strong managers against whom they would eventually turn. They express strong attachment to heroic stature and are frustrated by the loss of their heroic missions. A good example of the General type of departure style is marked by Lee Iaccoca's successful development of Chrysler followed by a brief retirement after which he attempted to undermine his hand-picked successor and reseat himself as CEO.

Ambassadors, in contrast to Monarchs and Generals, leave office gracefully. They are good at providing continuity and counsel for their successors.

Governors leave their companies for a limited term of office then, after retirement, move on to other challenges. They maintain very little ongoing contact with their companies after departure. An example of a Governor might be Bill Gutheridge who served as head coach of the University of North Carolina basketball program after Dean Smith's retirement. He served for a short period of time, maintained high standards, handled his stewardship duties well, and withdrew gracefully after a short time in favor of younger coaching candidates.

From empirical observation, there are not many Governors and Ambassadors as leaders of family businesses. Overwhelmingly, family business owners fall into the categories of Monarchs and Generals. Not to be indelicate, but family business owners are terrible at naming successors, grooming them, and exiting gracefully. Often, family business owners have to be figuratively dragged kicking and screaming from their thrones, and this determined reluctance to let go of power has negative ripple effects throughout the family and the business. Ironically, Monarchs acknowledged that after their retirements they could have done a much better job grooming their successors. Sonnenfeld also found that outside activities unrelated to the business are not fulfilling to retired CEOs. Charity work, board directorships, and other pursuits don't make up for the loss of heroic stature. The success that put the FBO on a pedestal makes it that much harder for him to find alternative means of maintaining his self esteem.

Irving Shapiro, former CEO of DuPont, had an interesting perspective for retiring CEOs. "Every CEO should remember that the position exists not for his benefit, but for the corporation's. It is his job to know when it is time to step down." Family business owners will be remembered for a host of accomplishments, the most enduring of which just might be the successful transition of their companies from one generation to the next. The sad thing is, because they hold on to the reins too long, most FBOs tarnish their reputations and harm their companies at the end of their tenures. They have a type of late career desperation to prove they are still young enough, smart enough, and vital enough to continue to imprint their companies and their communities. A graceful and pre-planned exit is an essential part of an FBO's legacy.

Keep Or Sell?

There has been a tremendous amount of discussion among family business commentators on the almost obsessive focus on successful succession of the family firm. Having a company is a powerful force in family life. It is often the focus of conversation around the dinner table or family gatherings. The closely held enterprise even pulls extended family into its gravitational field. Many times after the parent generation has died, the new family business leader assumes the leadership role in his family as "first among equals" among the siblings. When family business owners do their estate planning, family business succession is the most important topic of discussion; all other estate and tax counseling concepts are secondary. The family business, in short, has been the focus (if not the obsession) of the entrepreneur's daily life 24 hours a day for perhaps 30 or 40 years.

Keeping the business going is an obsession for many second generation family business children whether or not they are actually employed by the firm. In fact, in more than one series of family interviews, non-employee family members have stated they would quit their careers of 10 to 15 years if Mom or Dad needed them in the family business. These children would be willing to create upheaval in their own personal and professional lives in order to sustain the family company. However, experts are now raising the question of whether or not we spend too much time focusing on inter-family succession of the family enterprise rather than focusing on the success of the family business using a different measuring stick. Kenneth Kaye, in the September 1998 issue of *Family Business Review*, suggests that the new measure of success for a family company is the "amount of value added to next generation opportunity." Here are the questions nobody seems to ask:

- Is it the right thing for the family and the business to continue the enterprise into the second or third generation?
- Does that create the highest level of value added for future generations' opportunities?
- Where would the family members be most happy, successful, and fulfilled in their individual futures - inside the family business or pursuing opportunities elsewhere?
- What is the smartest choice to preserve harmony in future family generations - keeping the family company or selling it?

Family business owners must come to grips with the fact that selling or even closing down the family company *does not mean failure*. In many cases, selling or shutting the doors is the best thing to do given the specific circumstances. A slavish devotion to keeping the family business going can be foolish when the needs of the family and individual family members are taken into account. The obsession with succession is a barrier in many families to improved and lasting harmony and healthy communication.

A basic way to begin answering the keep or sell question is to develop a series of interrogatives:

- What is our collective vision for this family business?
- What is our collective vision for this family?
- Who in the family - if anyone - has the skills and leadership abilities necessary to lead the business in the future?
- Is the continuity of the family business really important?
- To whom is it important?

Analyzing the prospects for the successful future of the business requires a detailed examination of the industry, the management of the company, strengths of the company, weaknesses, opportunities for future growth, and threats from competition, regulation, etc. Some family business owners do not like to engage in long range strategic planning; however, the short term pain of doing an in-depth analysis far outweighs the long term misery that could be the result of a poorly thought out or non-existent succession strategy.

The Twelve Step Solution

With all the emotions, conflicting agendas, fear of change, and procrastination, how do family business owners transition themselves out of their carefully nurtured roles and into new ones befitting the dignity and prestige that they have earned?

Dr. James Lea cites a study of 42 entrepreneurial and family owned companies which attempted transition into the next generation. 14 of the 42 reported they started planning 10 years or more before making the transfer of management. Of that number, 86% of the companies were successfully operating 15 years later. 22 companies started planning between two and 10 years before making the transfer. There was a 50% survival rate among those firms. The remaining eight companies did not start planning soon enough, citing two years or less before handing over control. It is not surprising that 75% of these companies failed.

Dr. Leon Danco, in his *Twelve Commandments For The Business Owner*, devoted one-fourth of the commandments to specifics of succession. Commandments Eight through Ten read as follows:

- Thou shalt name thy successor.
- Thou shalt be responsible that thy successor be well taught.
- Thou shalt retire and install thy successor within thy powers within thy lifetime.

The family business owner has a covenant with his family, his enterprise, his employees, and his customers to see to it that the company continues into the next and future generations. It is essential that the FBO begin a structured process of letting go and preparing for succession. The following is a 12 step solution to successful family business succession.

Step One: Understand the Importance

It can't be stated often enough: The most important responsibility of a truly great leader is to pass the baton to the next leader. A living testimonial to the entrepreneur is how well the business survives without him. The current leader must believe that his number one priority and responsibility is to help the next leader or group of leaders get a successful start. Until the owner of the family enterprise truly understands and accepts this responsibility, there will be little or no chance for success and transition.

Step Two: Decide When To Leave

Determine when the current FBO wants to have the freedom to step away from the daily operations of his business. For maximum effectiveness, there needs to be at least five years and probably 10 before the transfer of authority. This gives the current leader time to phase himself out and phase in new leaders. For example, the current FBO might decide to cut back to a four-day work week in two years. In year four, he might cut back to a three-day work week and cut back a day in each successive year until ultimately withdrawing from day-to-day management responsibilities.

Most FBOs seem to feel that the best age to turn over authority is between 60 and 65. This puts the successor generation in their 30s to early 40s. If there is no family successor apparent, consider this: a recent study by Marquette University's Center for Family Business reports that one in four family firms plans to name a non-family member as its CEO. Not insignificantly, exiting at that stage of life also means that the senior generation will have time to enjoy golf, travel, etc. before the inevitable pressures of time bring on health concerns that preclude an active lifestyle.

An essential element in Step Two is for the current FBO to give serious thought to what he will do in retirement. Most FBOs fail to do so and find themselves at loose ends within a short time after exiting their jobs. Most say they want to travel and play golf, but let's face it, they can't travel and play golf 60 hours a week for 52 weeks a year. Those activities simply won't fill up a life. Dr. John Ward flatly states that 50% of exiting FBOs will find a reason - real or contrived - to return to their businesses within two years of exit. This is most often the case when exiting FBOs have not developed a "second career" or a series of hobbies, interests, and avocations that inspire them and stir their passions.

Step Three: Develop a Financial Exit Strategy

One reason why many owners never retire is because they haven't figured out how to continue their standards of living without their annual salaries from the business. The FBO must answer some serious questions. How much money does she need in today's dollars in order to maintain her standard of living? What sources of capital are available and how much inflation adjusted dollars will these sources provide in the future? Will her financial or real assets grow over time in order to provide a satisfactory income stream? If not, what can be done to maintain the senior generation's standard of living? Good financial planning is essential in Step Three. Money is the most tangible component of family business success; according to some family business commentators, research shows that even a desire for power and control ranks below money as the root cause of family disputes over succession. The financial needs of the senior generation simply must be addressed in developing any business succession program.

Step Four: Identify the Successors

Before attempting to choose a successor, it is essential to determine what qualities, talents, and experiences the new leader should possess. In the March 1998 edition of *Family Business Review*, James Chrisman, Jess Chua, and Pramodita Sharma researched 485 family businesses. They focused on identifying and discussing attributes in eight categories:

1. Relationship to the current leader.
2. Relationships to other family members.
3. Family standing.
4. Competence.
5. Personality traits.
6. Current involvement in the family business.
7. Age of the potential successor.
8. Compatibility of goals with the current CEO.

In their survey, the average age of the firms was 38 years and the average number of employees was 108. Median revenues for the firms were $5.3 million. 42% of respondents were first generation family businesses and 97% of the families owned 50% or more of the responding company's equity. 85% of the respondents were male.

The authors rated a total of 30 attributes for potential successors, and all but four of the 30 attributes were rated higher than average in importance in choosing a successor. In other words, the survey respondents were trying to balance 26 different, sometimes conflicting, attributes in determining who their optimum successors should be!

Family business owners rated the age, gender, and birth order of the potential successors as relatively unimportant. Respect from employees was considered the third most desirable attribute, while respect from actively involved family members was rated eleventh. What this might tell us is that family business owners might put more stock in the opinions and evaluations of their employees than anyone expected. In fact, it may point out a need for company-wide studies to help determine who employees feel would be the best choice of succession candidates.

While respect from actively involved family members was rated eleventh, respect by non-employee family members was a distant nineteenth in importance. This is a clear indicator that the respondents felt that their employee family members were in a better position to evaluate succession candidates than non-employee members. It may also reflect a simple fact that employee family members are in frequent contact with family CEOs. Non-employee family members have less frequent contact and, therefore, less opportunity to voice their opinions.

In another surprising item, family business owners rated outside management experience for the potential successor as above average. This is surprising given the fact that there are many candidates for second generation leadership who have never worked outside their family companies. Outside employment of potential successors is becoming more common, but is hardly the rule.

The respondents identified integrity and commitment to the business as the two most desirable attributes; in fact, these two attributes were rated significantly higher than any others. Integrity refers to moral fiber and character; family business owners consider character to be the best determinant of a person's value. A close second was commitment to the business. Commitment to the business has often been characterized by family business owners as "passion," a "fire in the belly," or " whatever it takes." Family business owners are nothing if not dedicated to their companies.

Other important attributes were decision-making abilities, experience, and interpersonal skills. The authors interpreted the relative rankings to mean that while family firms view interpersonal skills as important, without integrity they consider interpersonal skills "slick" and ineffective in the long run. Intelligence, self confidence, and creativity were also highly rated.

This is an interesting study that provides insight into what family business owners look for in evaluating their successors. However, it leaves quite a bit to be desired in terms of specificity. It also points out that choosing a successor in a family business is still much more art than science.

In order to begin your quest for finding a successor, you must define the CEO job clearly. Developing your vision for the company and a specific organizational chart are exceptional steps here. The current CEO must also develop a skills inventory to establish criteria for leading the company. These exercises mean that your business must be professionalized. Successors must be identified, groomed, and trained to take over. They should not be thrust into the executive decision-making chair without a period of proper education and preparation. Leadership development and individual coaching to improve weak spots are essential. For example, many family business owners report that their children are weak in understanding financial statements and other financial aspects of the company. A period of formal training to improve this common weak area is an example of the type of training your successors will need in order to take the your company to the next level.

Step Five: Begin the Silent Phase

During the silent phase, only your professional advisors and closest managers are made aware of the succession plan. Because of the necessary development of plans, essential people must be brought into your thinking; however, the number should not be more than absolutely necessary. In the event that the anointed successor doesn't meet expectations or doesn't progress as originally envisioned, there will be a "no harm-no foul" consequence. If the world knows of your plan and also knows the plan didn't work, the FBO and his anointed successor will be embarrassed and perhaps even suffer unwanted business consequences.

Step Six: Write the Succession Plan

Develop a written plan with a timeline of five to 10 years. This plan will outline the different positions and responsibilities that the successor should fill within the company. It will include a timetable with trigger dates which will set out progressions. For example, the successor might take over marketing on a certain date and add accounting responsibilities on a subsequent date.

An important element in this process is to give the potential successor profit responsibility for a department, division, project, or branch as soon as possible. It is important that progress be evaluated in as many ways as possible. Numerical mileposts and benchmarks are extremely valuable.

Finally, this plan should discuss how and when to begin the transfer of stock ownership in the company. Don't worry if all the details aren't nailed down at the very beginning or if you stray a little from your timeline. During the 10 year succession period, there will be time to modify and improve on the plan. The goal should be that the successor should have day-to-day operating control of the company early enough to insure an approximate 20 year tenure as leader. This means your successor leader should be around 40 to 45 years old at the time of ascension.

Step Seven: Develop A Business Plan

It is imperative that the current leader and the successor jointly develop a plan for the future of the business. The current leader must participate in the process but cannot be allowed to dominate. He knows what has happened historically and perhaps has the best perspective of today's operations, but he cannot and should not dictate the future direction.

There are several clear advantages to this procedure. First, the two leaders should develop a closer business relationship by forging a joint plan for the future direction of the company. Second, the current leader will gain a greater comfort level with his successor if he knows where things are headed and will be much less likely to second guess or criticize upon his departure. After all, he was a major architect of the plan. Third, the successor will gain invaluable knowledge and perspective about the company. Fourth, knowing that a carefully crafted plan is in place to smooth the transition will raise his comfort level at takeover time. Fifth, employees, bankers, suppliers, and customers can take comfort in the fact that a plan exists to keep their profitable business alliances in place and operating smoothly.

Working in concert, the current and future leaders must craft a plan with as much detail as possible just as though the business was going to borrow a substantial sum of money and the business plan was built to convince bankers to make a loan. The business plan should contain a brief history of your company, the keys to your success, a break-even analysis, and your current and potential customers. The plan should discuss what you are selling, what your niche market is, your sales forecast, your marketing plan, biographies on your management team, profit and loss expectations, cash flow projections, projected balance sheets, target business ratios, sales targets, and a history of past performance. It is also helpful to include an evaluation of strengths, weaknesses, opportunities, and threats (a SWOT evaluation).

Will your projections turn out according to plan? No, of course not. However, outcomes will be much more predictable than if there was no prescribed course, and the future leader will have a much greater ability to adapt to contingencies than he would have had in the absence of a plan.

Step Eight: Appoint A Family Business Advisory Board

The purpose of the board is to get to know the current leader as well the chosen successor. In addition, the board must learn about the company's philosophy, vision, challenges, and opportunities.   It is desirable that the board have a minimum of two years to get to know the personalities of the current leader as well as the future leader prior to execution of the succession plan.

Depending on the needs of the business and the desire of the current and future leaders, the family business advisory board step could be achieved in one of two ways.   The first could be an executive committee formed within the company consisting of department heads. The second method would be to have outside advisors. Outside members could include someone from a related industry, a respected community business leader, or someone with specialized, helpful skills in the areas of international trade, labor relations, technology, etc.   The number of outside advisors is not important, but there should be enough so there is an uneven number of board members. The board should meet three to four times per year, and outside members should be compensated for their time and travel expenses.

There is the desire on the part of some family business owners to include their CPA, lawyer, banker, or other business advisors, but the best advice is not to compromise their loyalties. You already pay them for their professional advice; why does it make sense to appoint them to the family business advisory board and pay them twice for the same advice? They should sit in on advisory board meetings so that you can have the benefit of their professional thinking; however, they should be compensated as family business advisors, not as members of the board.

Many family business owners recoil at the idea of having a board tell them how to run their businesses. Please keep in mind this is an *advisory* board. They can't possibly tell you what to do! If they did get into a conflict posture with you, you could simply disband the board. These people are there to help you overcome sticky family and business situations. Their advice and experience will allow you to leverage your own experience and vision as a business leader. Most family business owners who have created a family business advisory board say that it is the most positive step they have ever taken in lifting their businesses to the next level.

Step Nine: Announce the Plan

When the successor leader's progress is sufficient and the necessary plans are in place, announce the plan to the family, the public, etc. This announcement might be made two to four years after the initial implementation. It puts everyone on notice who the successor is and indicates that a formal transition will occur according to a specific timeline.

Step Ten: Announce the Transfer Date

Announce the formal date of transfer of operating control. This should be no more than 12 to 18 months away from the actual transfer. Now the world will know when the current leader plans to turn over the reins and puts everyone on notice that allegiances must be shifted. It also prevents the current leader from backing away from his commitment to shift into a new, different role in the organization.

Additionally, the succession of the future leader is a great opportunity to get positive publicity for your business. Local newspapers are always fascinated by transfers of power and compelling success stories for family businesses. Take the opportunity to get as much as you can out of this succession plan by putting media resources at your disposal for free publicity.

Step Eleven: Pass the Baton

Much like runners in a relay race, the current leader has been running hard for many years. The successor has been getting up to speed so that a smooth handoff of the baton will insure the momentum continues. If everything up to this step has been done correctly, the actual transfer should be a non-event. However, if the future leader hasn't begun sprinting to get up to speed, a collision of titanic proportions can occur, and the future of the business and the family could be in doubt.

Step Twelve: Transfer Ownership Control

This is one of the most important elements of the plan. Nothing could be more devastating than to have the retired leader come back and boldly announce that he is retaking the throne. This happens frequently, and is unfair to both generations of leaders. Transferring more than 50% of the voting stock of the company assures that the past leader moves on to the role of elder statesman, and the successor properly takes his place as the quarterback of the team.

If this 12 step planning process seems like a great deal of work, it is. Some FBOs will be so concerned about getting every last detail in place they won't ever get started on developing the plan. Don't be concerned if you don't know every answer to every question in the beginning; few ever see the final picture before starting to paint. You can be assured that a successful transition will never take place unless you start. The founder will ultimately be remembered and judged by both family and history based on his ability to successfully turn his job over to someone else.

Conclusion

Successor leaders in the family company must create new relationships with their parents. These new relationships cannot evolve naturally out of the biological family; the business demands that this evolution have a different set of rules. There are several factors which are related to positive experiences in intergenerational transfers of family companies:

1. The relationships must be based on mutual respect and

acknowledgment of each individual's unique role in the business.

2. The successor leader needs to have clear authority and responsibility within the business, a sense of accomplishment, and active participation in the continuing growth and development of the company.

3. The successor needs to have a sense of equality with the parent, and both generations need a structured mechanism to discuss and resolve conflict.

4. The successor needs the training necessary for business success.

The 12 step program outlined above can put most family business owners on a fast track to a positive, successful exit and a mutually rewarding succession for their family enterprises.

CHAPTER EIGHT

HOW MUCH IS TOO MUCH?
HOW SOON IS TOO SOON?

PRESCRIPTION: Provide for the distribution of the wealth you have created in a way that does not retard or undermine your children's opportunities to become valuable, productive members of society.

1. Your children need to know what is expected of them to be eligible to enter your business. Develop specific *entry rules* so everyone's expectations will be aligned both before and after they begin employment.
2. Your success may have created wealth beyond your wildest dreams. Recognize that your wealth may actually prove to be an emotional burden to your offspring. Decide *how much is too much and how soon* is too soon for your children.
3. Your spouse needs to know what to do and who to call about your affairs after returning home from your funeral. Develop a specific *get home from the funeral plan.*

"For a person of wealth to think of handing it down to a child is almost like handing down a gun...Inherited wealth does more harm than good...It eats away at your self-esteem. More people resent you than admire you. You never know who is approaching you for what agenda."

Swanee Hunt,
daughter of H.L. Hunt
Parade Magazine, November 30, 1997

Coping with family business success can be a real challenge for even the most well rounded business families. As an example, how many times have you heard your children or children of other family business owners struggle with ambivalent feelings about money and the success of their families of origin? A family business owner told the story of his son's junior high school friend who visited their substantial new home. "Gosh," the visitor exclaimed, "you must be rich." The son of the family business owner came to Mom and Dad genuinely curious: "Mom and Dad, are we rich?" The son simply never thought of himself or his family as anything other than average, hard working, middle class folks.

Another example: A young woman attended the university named after her great, great grandfather who started the school over 100 years ago. When curious classmates asked "Are you related to...," she was struck with conflicting feelings of pride and remorse. On various occasions she said, no, an out and out lie, or equivocated by saying, "yes, but..." It seemed that it was easier to deny the truth of her family's accomplishments than admit it to her peers.

Let's face it; in our society there is a hostile envy towards those who have achieved real wealth. The irony is that the same people who are resented for their money are generally admired for their industry, thrift, and ambition. The truth is that people who have achieved business success in America are the most productive creators of jobs, useful services and technologies, and ideas that improve the lives of others. In spite of this fact, one has only to pick up a newspaper, magazine, or watch the six o'clock news to hear some veiled or overt attack on "the rich." It is worse for the kids of family business owners. Think about people who refer to your children or grandchildren as members of the "lucky sperm club" or call them "trust fund babies." These remarks are demeaning and insulting - imagine the psychological impact it can have on people hit with these pejoratives. Often the children of successful family business owners are exposed to this societal envy when they are young, and it carries through adulthood. This type of treatment can leave serious scars, and in some extreme cases, it can even cause children to resent the family members who made the inherited wealth possible.

Even where the prejudices about wealth are absent, inherited wealth can be a curse upon individual business family members. Having too much money, especially money that an individual did not have to work to earn, can create aimlessness and rob one of the need to be a productive member of society. Today, at the dawn of an unprecedented transfer of wealth between generations, family business owners are struggling with the question of how much is too much and when is too soon for their heirs to reap the benefits of lifetimes of hard work. FBOs want their businesses to continue and their children to be productive human beings. They *don't* want their children to be destitute and lead lives of desperation; however, they realize that inherited wealth can be a poison to an individual's motivation and work ethic. Inherited wealth can even undermine a grown, mature child's sense of perspective.

Most family business owners have three simple goals for their wealth beyond just keeping the family firm in business. First, the FBO wants to protect his family from destitution; he wants a family safety net for medical emergencies, education of grandchildren, etc. Second, FBOs want to provide opportunities to their family members. For example, many family business owners value entrepreneurial characteristics, but they know how hard it is to take risks and get a fledgling business off the ground. They may want to provide "seed money" to build an entrepreneurial idea into a real business. Third, most family business owners *do not want* to provide a carefree lifestyle for their heirs. Rugged family business owners know that giving a large subsidy to heirs can often take away their motivation for self improvement.

It is difficult to grow up in a family business. Some family business commentators have said that it is nearly impossible for a family business son or daughter to develop an independent sense of identity. Others have said that inherited affluence can infantilize heirs. There is a syndrome some psychologists call "affluenza" where family business heirs never develop a sense of their own strengths, meaningful commitments, or abilities to come to terms with their inherited wealth.

Still other family business commentators turn to mythology for an explanation of why it is difficult to grow up in a family company. Mythological heroes have to leave home. Their journeys begin when they wake up to their task and leave their families of origin to begin their journeys of life-threatening challenges which require them to reach deep inside for hidden strengths. These mythological quests develop the hero's inner talents. Dr. Dennis Jaffe, author of *Working With The Ones You Love*, says that "the family business sometimes does a strange job of short-circuiting personal development by making a seductive offer to the hero to stay at home and not grow." In other words, family business children are seduced into staying home to work in the family company and consequently forfeit their opportunities to wander into the unknown and develop their own independent senses of heroic achievement.

Sometimes it's success itself which creates problems. This may be counterintuitive because in our society it is generally seen that success is the positive resolution of a lifetime's struggle for achievement. However, success is not an end unto itself. Success brings with it its own set of problems and new challenges. This chapter can help you and your business family cope with the challenges of success and provide a road map so your lifetime achievements are not marred by "affluenza" or other pathologies of success.

How Much Is Too Much? How Soon Is Too Soon?

You've all seen it. Everyone can think of examples from their own communities of children or grandchildren of wealthy lineage who have affluent lifestyles and plenty of money, but who are morally bankrupt, lead aimless, wandering personal lives, or spend their days in search of the next alcohol or drug fix. What thoughts and feelings race through your mind when you think about these people? How are they viewed by the community and society at large? Most families consider it a great privilege to be able to pass along wealth to their heirs, but in many cases the double edged sword of inherited wealth creates more problems then benefits.

How much is too much? Two men who are among the richest people on earth have made their philosophies on inherited wealth clear. Bill Gates, founder and chairman of Microsoft, said he is going to leave his children a relatively minor inheritance and give the rest of his vast fortune to charity. Warren Buffet, the billionaire investor, has a similar philosophy. Buffet has been quoted as saying, "The perfect inheritance is enough money so they feel they can do anything, but not so much they can do nothing."

Family business owners worry about spoiling their children if they give them too much too soon. Dr. Tom Stanley has done some research into the effect of gifts on the recipients, and he says that "It cannot be denied that adult children who receive cash gifts differ from

131

those who do not." His research demonstrates that in eight of 10 occupational categories, gift receivers have smaller levels of net worth (wealth) than those who do not receive gifts.   Large subsidies may create a sense of entitlement in the receivers and cause them to be less focused, productive, and hard working than their non-gift receiving peers.

Dr. Stanley draws several conclusions about gifts and recipients:

1. Giving precipitates more consumption than saving and investing.
2. Gift receivers, in general, never fully distinguish between their wealth and the wealth of their gift-giving parents.
3. Gift receivers are significantly more dependent on credit than are non-receivers.
4. Receivers of gifts invest much less money than non-receivers.

Dr. Stanley refers to children of affluent parents who become dependent on cash gifts and other subsidies as people who receive "economic outpatient care."   Most family business owners value the rugged traits which allow them to become successful in the first place: integrity, hard work, thrift, service to others, discipline, honesty, etc. Ironically, their success and the gifts they are economically able to make may serve to undermine these desirable character traits in their own children.

As we saw before, most family business owners have three simple goals for their wealth:

1. Protect the family from destitution.
2. Provide opportunities to family members.
3. They *do not* want to provide non-working lifestyles to their heirs.

How can FBOs accomplish those three somewhat mutually exclusive goals simultaneously? The first step is to be open and honest with your children or grandchildren about issues for handling societal prejudice against wealth.

1. Tell the truth about your economic conditions. It is not always necessary to disclose actual numbers, but if you have a substantial home, vacation homes at the coast and the mountains, a company with multiple locations, and are constantly being sought out by non-profit organizations and other entities for your expertise, there is no point in poor mouthing your circumstances and telling your children you are living hand to mouth. It serves no purpose to deny the fact that you have been incredibly successful by most people's standards.

2. Put a substantial amount of money into the hands of the children and let them manage it (define what you mean by substantial on the basis of your family's net worth). Seek and consider their opinions about money and treat them in a way that builds their own self-worth. Who knows, given a little bit of opportunity for creativity, you may find you have another Warren Buffet or Bill Gates in your family. Monitor the progress of your children in managing their funds. If one or more is having difficulty, discuss the matter and develop positive alternatives for moving forward.

3. Embrace reality. There cannot be denial or rationalizations about your success. Only when you are yourself will your children have an opportunity to become themselves and develop well adjusted and self-actualized personalities.

4. Draw boundaries. Teach your children to say that the success of your family or your family business is a private matter. That sends a clear message that it is truly not of the business of any one who is not an employee, stockholder, customer, or vendor to the business. A privately owned business is just that - private.

5. Use humor. Humor is the equalizer and diffuses many

133

potentially tense or uncomfortable situations. Teaching your children to use humor to deflect societal envy or reverse discrimination when it appears will help them develop greater perspective and is a useful tactic for handling critical or envious people.

These ground rules can help children of successful family business owners to cope with a phenomenon that is not regularly addressed or even admitted in our society. Reverse discrimination and hostile envy towards wealthy people is a real phenomenon, and your children must be educated to handle this uncomfortable reality.

What other tools are there for a family business owner to go about encouraging and rewarding responsible financial behavior in his children? One of the great tools for encouraging valuable, noble, and productive behavior is called the Family Incentive Trust™. The Family Incentive Trust™ encourages responsible behavior by future generations in your family. It can help minimize conflict in future family generations over who gets what in terms of inheritances. It can help foster a sense of family cohesiveness and mission by encouraging charitable behavior. It can provide money to sponsor family retreats or smaller family meetings periodically to help the family work on improving communications, closeness, and goal setting. There are literally dozens of things that a Family Incentive Trust™ can do to encourage responsible behavior.

What a Family Incentive Trust™ *cannot* do is assure good descendants; there is no tool to assure that. However, what the Family Incentive Trust™ can do is help make sure that children who would have been good are not turned to the dark side by their inherited wealth. It also gives protection and opportunities to future generations which could have been squandered if an inheritance was taken down by a lavish, consumption oriented lifestyle.

The Family Incentive Trust™ is based on the economic fact that if you subsidize something, you get more of it. The first purpose of the Family Incentive Trust™ is to provide a safety net for the family. The second purpose is to provide family incentives for responsible, productive behavior. Finally, the Trust can function as a private family bank or family charitable device. Generally speaking, the incentives should be of a positive nature. Negative incentives are not recommended because they can be counterproductive and create conflict among heirs. The incentives should be consistent with the deep, heartfelt values of the family. The incentives should help develop character and provide opportunities. They must be communicated regularly to all the members of the family so the heirs will know what rewards are available to them as they develop their personal aspirations.

One of the most frequently used incentives is the earned income match which encourages work among younger family members. For example, a work incentive might read that the trust will "match 100% of the earned income of any beneficiary under age 24, not to exceed $2,000 per year (increased by the Consumer Price Index)." Another incentive can provide income so that two parents don't have to work to make ends meet. For example, one can say that the trust would distribute $20,000 a year to any parent who stays at home with a minor child. Another widespread incentive is to provide for the education of family members. Other incentives can provide for post-secondary education, religious training, scouting, testing for drugs and alcohol, achieving good grades, graduating from a certain level of school, or a one time family trip to the Holy Land. Every family can literally create its own list of incentives consistent with their values and family missions.

The Family Incentive Trust™ is a beautiful way for a successful, high net worth family business owner to encourage and perpetuate the values that allowed him to be successful. This concept can help family business owners transform the potential poison of inherited wealth into a magic potion which will encourage and reward responsible behavior for generations to come; it is a valuable tool in building your family legacy.

Entry Rules for Family Businesses

The following is a family business scenario that comes up over and over again. The family company is cruising along at a nice growth rate with significant profits. Of the founding owner's three children, one elected to come into the family enterprise after a brief post-college career. The other two children pursued other educational and career paths with their parents' blessings. The employee sibling has climbed the corporate ladder, has put in 10 years of her life towards making the family business healthy and profitable, and has engineered a program of gradual change and modernization so that the business is poised to move into the next decade. Suddenly, things begin to spin out of control. The youngest child in the family, eight years younger than the eldest, returns to the hometown after being dismissed from his job on the west coast. The circumstances surrounding the dismissal are murky at best. The youngest child attended several different colleges and never collected a diploma from any. Since leaving college, he bounced around from job to job and city to city always looking to Mom and Dad for financial and emotional support. Now he is home and appears at the office Monday morning to see his father. His comment is, "Dad, I'm home. I am ready to enter the family business. Where is my office?"

What is Dad to do? What problems could arise from the baby of the family showing up and requesting a position of responsibility in the family business? How is the oldest child going to feel about her baby brother's entry, knowing that she has put in 10 years of blood, toil, sweat, and tears? What do Mom and Dad do about their estate plans? How do they balance the ultimate inheritances of the three children?

Researchers Astrachan and Kolenko in a 1994 study found that only 16% of family businesses had formal, established entry requirements for family members. In a 1993 survey, Arthur Andersen learned that three out of four have no formal policy regarding qualifications for family members to be employed in the business full time.

The statistics paint a picture. Parents want their children to participate in the family enterprise for a host of reasons. However, only 16% to 25% have formal policies to determine eligibility for entering the family company under certain circumstances. It is a bit inconsistent, isn't it?

Family businesses with multiple second or third generation candidates who could work for the company should have formal, written entry rules. These rules can head off some of the ugliest family disputes. There is nothing more devastating to the harmony of a family than having brothers and sisters battle over which sons, daughters, nieces, or nephews have the right (or wrong) strengths and talents to become the next CEO of the firm.

Good entry rules should specify the ages at which family members will be allowed to participate in the business. They should specify the education requirements for family members. Most family business counselors believe that children who are going to enter the management of a family company should have significant outside work experience (usually five years or more) and should have left their previous employers in good standing with track records of success and promotion. The entry rules should specify minimum standards of personal conduct. For example, no family business should want to hire a family member who has a drug or alcohol addiction. It may be tempting to give that family member a job to "keep him off the streets," but unless the family member is capable of giving a full day's work in exchange for a day's pay, he will be a drain on, not a benefit to, the business. Some family businesses require a certain amount of civic or community service, some relationship to a community church, or other types of stewardship behavior.

The family business should not create a position for a family member unless the growth of the business demands it. In other words, it is the wrong thing to do - and the wrong message to send to your other employees - to create a "make work" job for a family member just so he can have something to do during the daytime.

The position contract for the newly hired family member should specify the daily work hours expected from the employee. Family members are not entitled to excessive vacation or travel; they should be held to the same standards as other employees. There should be measurable performance standards and specific, scheduled times for periodic performance reviews. In most family companies, it is a good idea to see to it that the family member will not be reviewed by another family member; if possible, the new entrant should be supervised by a non-family employee of the business.

Management should lay out a career track for the aspiring family member. If a family member knows prior to taking a position that the path he most desires in his own career is blocked for one reason or another, he may find the job much less appealing. The entry rules and job description should cover specialized, industry-specific training for the family member. Compensation should be spelled out in advance and should not be more than what the market would pay for a non-family member in the same position. Generally, trade associations are great places to find out what various jobs with various responsibilities pay in the marketplace. There are also several websites which can provide salary information by industry and region.

Entry rules can be very detailed or could be somewhat abbreviated. The most important thing is that the family company has entry rules *in writing*. The family can make clear in Family Council or Board meetings that these entry rules exist, they will be enforced fairly and equitably, and that there will be no exceptions. Informality abounds in family businesses, and sometimes it is that very informality that causes dissension and upheaval in the family. Written entry rules for your family company can go a long way towards eliminating some of the fuel that creates the fire of conflict.

What Will Your Family Do When They Get Home From Your Funeral?

No one likes to think of it. No one wants to imagine what life would be like if we were to have to go on without our spouses, best friends, and lovers. Let's face it: that is the reality. In a famous line from *The Outlaw Josey Wales*, "dying is a part of living."

Aside from the shock and emotional trauma inherent in losing the most significant person in your life, how would you feel about your financial security and your ability to carry on the family, household, and business? To whom would you go for advice? How would you want your children to remember you? How would you want your employees to remember you? What does your will say, and when was the last time it was updated? Do you even know the location of your will? What is your normal monthly personal cash flow? How is your departure likely to affect that cash flow? To whom do you owe money, and what are your monthly obligations with respect to your personal and business creditors? These questions are all vital to a surviving spouse who will be faced, maybe for the first time, with dealing with all the realities, business and personal, that two people have worked together to handle in the past.

The usual arrangement in most families is that one or the other - but not both - of the spouses handles the family's finances and organization. That individual knows the details about the checking accounts, which banks they are in, where the retirement money is invested, the location of the wills, the location of the insurance policies, etc. In virtually all cases, that individual keeps the information in his head by mutual agreement of both spouses. It is just simpler for one person to handle that particular family responsibility while the other spouse handles other family responsibilities more suited to his or her temperament, personality, interest, and level of attention to detail.

This typical scenario with one severely under-informed spouse is a recipe for disaster. Can you imagine the unnecessary burden placed on a grieving spouse at the most emotionally vulnerable time of her life? Not knowing the source of next month's mortgage payment is a horrifying burden to face when every other aspect of the family routine is torn apart.

Family business owners face a unique burden. In addition to all the other personal and family trauma caused by the death of a loved one, they have tens to thousands of employees who depend on their abilities to make strong and swift business decisions. Throwing a grieving spouse into a business decision-making role without sufficient discussion and preparation is a punishment no one should have to face. Family business owners should develop an organization and plan that will allow both spouses (and adult children) to know such basic things as the location of the wills (and what is in them) and how much money it takes to run the household. Family members should be prepared with information that will allow them to notify key people related to the family and the business such as the CPA, attorney, banker, and insurance agent. They will need to quickly contact the key employees of the family business who will be facing greater responsibility for operations in the short run. If the stock in the business is subject to a buy-sell agreement, family members should know where the document is, what it says, and what steps need to be taken with the company's professional advisors to fulfill its terms.

Every surviving spouse should have a clear picture of what kind of financial obligations exist, what monthly cash flow he can expect, and how much money it takes to live the current lifestyle. He should also know what irregular expenditures are likely to pop up (quarterly tax payments, gifts related to estate planning, insurance premiums, property taxes, club membership dues, etc.). The survivor needs to know where the original insurance policies are and the procedures for notifying the companies about death claims. The survivor should know where all the investments are. It is quite common for family business owners to have brokerage accounts with multiple investment houses. If that is the case, the survivor needs the name of the brokerage company, the name of the broker, all account numbers, and approximate account balances. The same is true for bank statements and the company pension or retirement plans.

Where are the valuable papers and records of other valuable assets kept? For example, where are the titles to your automobiles or recreational vehicles? Where are the deeds to property that is owned by the family? Are there collectibles (i.e. art collections, stamp collections, coin collections, gun collections, etc.)? Where are your other important papers like your birth certificates and your marriage certificate? Do you have other things about which the family members should know? For example, how can people get into your computer files? Do you use passwords? If there is a safe in your home or office, who else has the combination?

None of us likes to think about the possibility of our own demise;

however, that demise is inevitable. Adding to the burden of a grieving family by being sloppy, disorganized, or simply uncommunicative with our spouses is a sin no one - much less a family business owner - should commit. Plan for what your family will do when they get home from your funeral.

Conclusion

Family business owners have a unique burden in providing for the equitable distribution of the opportunities and wealth they have created. For your family members, whether they are employees or not, wealth can be a two-edged sword. No successful family business owner relishes the thought of his children leading aimless, nonproductive lives because the first or second generation family success made that lifestyle possible. Developing open communication including frequent family meetings, family retreats, and open discussions about money and the responsibilities associated with it goes a long way toward making the creation of wealth positive rather than a curse which undermines the abilities of certain family members to function as solid citizens.

It is important that successor generation family members have entry rules which clearly lay out in a fair and unbiased way the criteria for entering the family company. For some families, the business exists to serve the family, and, if an individual has the right last name, family members are guaranteed employment. For other families, the family exists to serve the business, and only those who can contribute in a real way to the mission of the organization are eligible to be employees of the organization. The vast majority of family business owners want to fall in the latter category and generally abide by that philosophy. However, in times of distress for one or more family members, they find ways to make exceptions to the rule and, at least temporarily, they fall back into the former philosophy. A good way to help clarify the expectations and opportunities for second, third, or fourth generation members of your family is to have specific, clearly defined, written entry rules.

Finally, after a lifetime of great works, a family business owner needs to instruct his family on what needs to be done when they get home from his funeral. With their senses of heroic mission and heroic stature, family business owners often have trouble grasping the concept of their own mortality. Eventually, however, they do, and they hire professionals to help them develop estate plans. In virtually 100% of the cases, however, the estate plan is not accompanied by an organization plan that puts all of the testamentary documents, business agreements, names, addresses, and phone numbers for key parties for notification, financial records, and cash flow information together in one place in a structured way for the benefit of grieving family members. It is not enough to simply draft documents, execute them, and file them away in a desk drawer somewhere. It is important to organize your information in a coherent way so that your family members won't spend the first 30 days after your death scrambling to comply with the demands of bankers, creditors, employees, and others. You can provide a positive influence on the way they remember you by leaving your affairs in a tidy, organized way and by thinking through all the material items they will need to carry on after you're gone. The ultimate test of a good steward is how he leaves his family and business after he is gone and how well they function as a group in his absence. Developing a specific "get home from the funeral plan" can be the final determinant on the quality of your stewardship to your family and your business.

CHAPTER NINE

THE CHANGE MODEL

PRESCRIPTION: Understanding that change is inevitable, transform yourself and your organization from focusing on maintaining the status quo to learning, continually growing, and seeking new opportunities for improvement.

In public speaking appearances we often demonstrate the anxiety associated with change with a simple exercise. We ask the people on either side of the room to stand up, leave their belongings in place, and move to a new seat on the opposite side of the room. This request is usually met with blank stares followed by grumbling, nervous laughter, gradual, halfhearted acceptance, and some outright noncompliance. When folks have moved a few feet away from their original seats, we shout, "STOP!" Everyone then returns to his original seat. After they've resettled, we review the experience of reacting to a request for change. People talk about the feelings they had upon being requested to move: butterflies in the stomach, uncertainly over whether or not their belongings were safe, wonder where they'd find themselves on the other side of the room, concern over leaving the familiar people on either side of them for unfamiliar people in a new location, concern over whether there'd be a glass of water at their new location, etc. The point of the exercise is to identify the reactions, most of which are quite negative, even when the change itself is rather insignificant. If there's resistance and negative emotion associated with an insignificant change, what type of emotional reactions and resistance are family businesses likely to experience when asked to change the way they've conducted themselves and their businesses for the last 20 years?

Change is a dirty word in most family companies. People who are attracted to owning and managing their own businesses tend to like steadiness, predictability, plans made well in advance, and seeing clearly what the near future holds. They don't like sudden changes in plans, sudden shifts in business or family environments, unpredictability, and continually changing requests or demands on them. In general, family business owners don't like change and react negatively to it.

Change is real, inevitable, and the pace of change is *accelerating*. This chapter seeks to provide a graphic model and a clear explanation of the various steps associated with change so that it becomes a less fearful prospect and one that can be dealt with intellectually and practically rather than emotionally and fearfully.

The Change Model

The change model was originally developed by the late, renowned family therapist Virginia Satir. It was subsequently built upon and expanded by practitioners like Jean McLendon. The Satir change model is a powerful and helpful way to look at change in businesses and organizations. It graphically describes what it feels like to be in a process of change and also identifies the discrete steps that need to take place in order for a change to be successful. When change (resulting in chaos) is introduced into the family business environment, most people are ill prepared to receive the changes and react in a negative or dysfunctional way which makes the change that much more difficult to implement. The negative cycle builds upon itself, and eventually people or an organization atrophy and become highly resistant to change.

Virginia Satir believed that much of human behavior is learned, and functional behavior can be learned to take the place of dysfunctional behavior. People want to change even though they may be resistant. Resistance is a natural, human reaction - it's less threatening to stay with a familiar way of doing things than risk venturing into the unknown. The change model helps people visualize more of their possibilities or choices. Satir believed that people often resist change because they no longer see themselves as having choices. This model, then, can be effective in helping family business leaders and change agents get people comfortable with the introduction of new ways of doing things and transform their organizations from those obsessed with maintaining the old status quo into vital, learning organizations that readily embrace change and seek to make change a part of their business growth culture.

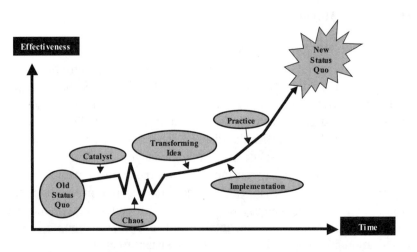

Sources: Satir Systems Development Programs, Jean McLendon

The seven steps in the change model are:

1. Old Status Quo
2. Catalyst
3. Chaos
4. Transforming Idea
5. Implementation
6. Practice
7. New Status Quo

We will examine each of the seven change stages in turn.

Old Status Quo

Old status quo is like a magnet. It's an area of comfort, known and familiar, like your home or an old pair of shoes. Finding ourselves in a state of change and in an area of discomfort, uncertainty, or reduction, human nature causes us to want to revert to the old status quo which is characterized by belonging, identity, and stability. People attach real or imagined survival value to old status quo even if it's genuinely harmful. Status quo doesn't mean that people aren't doing anything positive or moving forward incrementally. It simply means they're doing it the same way they've done it before. A common business term for status quo these days is "comfort zone."

Performance in a company at this stage could be flat, improving, or going backwards. Some of the feelings that old status quo can evoke include:

Positive Emotions	Negative Emotions
• Security	• Boredom
• Comfort	• Restlessness
• Peace	• Dissatisfaction
• Restfulness	• Tiredness
• Confidence	• Uncertainty
• Satisfaction	
• Warmth	
• Seduction	
• Friendliness	

The positive emotions are longer and more compelling list than the negative emotions. It's easy to see why old status quo is so magnetic.

Catalyst

The catalyst is the motivator for changing the status quo. It can also be referred to as a foreign element that requires a response. The catalyst or foreign element could be a person, an event, or forced change from outside the organization; it's the motivator for changing the old status quo. It frightens the majority of the people in the system.

It threatens to undermine the familiar, stable teams that they've enjoyed for so long. The wide range of emotions involved at this stage include:

Positive Emotions	Negative Emotions
• Excitement	• Fear
• Exhilaration	• Frustration
	• Despair
	• Anger
	• Anxiety
	• Pressure
	• Confusion
	• Uncertainty
	• Unpredictability
	• Dizziness

The negative emotions block the abilities of the people involved in the change to see positive outcomes. Survival mechanisms kick in, and people express a desire to eliminate the pressure of the foreign element.

Chaos

Chaos is brought on by an impending change because, while there is a catalyst, there's no previously known solution or path to the solution. The period of chaos is usually relatively short but could extend all the way to new status quo (or new comfort level) or until reversion to the old status quo. This is the period where it's easiest to revert to the old status quo because it's still familiar and relatively close while the vision of the new status quo seems distant and is not clear.

The same emotions apply to this period as to the catalyst period, and they may vary widely. Likewise, performance may vary widely and is often negative, reinforcing desire to go back to old status quo.

Positive Emotions	Negative Emotions
• Excitement	• Fear
• Exhilaration	• Frustration
	• Despair
	• Anger
	• Anxiety
	• Pressure
	• Confusion
	• Uncertainty
	• Unpredictability
	• Dizziness

The human experience of chaos is one of loss and panic. People behave differently and uncharacteristically as they resort to basic survival behavior. That behavior may be passive resistance or even resemble outright rebellion in the face of change.

Transforming Idea

The transforming idea stage is the clarification of what the new status quo might look like and the plan of how to get there. The new idea carries excitement, relief, and comfort from chaos in the belief there'll be a positive outcome to the changes afoot. The idea and plan itself can instill confidence and satisfaction to the people involved in the change. Effectiveness often improves at this stage due to positive emotions and visions of positive outcomes. However, chaos still often abounds, and there can be continued decline in effectiveness at this stage because there's been no permanent change. It's still common to attempt to revert to old status quo if there's insufficient confidence in the plan or if the plan looks difficult or tedious to implement. Changes fail at this point due to either a lack of a plan or a poor planning process. The result of a failure of the transforming idea is a return to old status quo.

<u>Positive Emotions</u>	<u>Negative Emotions</u>
• Excitement	• Fear
• Exhilaration	• Anxiety
• Confidence	• Uncertainty

The transforming idea enables people in the system to accept the catalyst and see, perhaps for the first time, how it can work for them. New behaviors begin to take place and performance, while still often erratic, begins to improve. The transforming idea triggers a kind of euphoria in the group, and they begin to feel invincible and ecstatic about the new possibilities. There's still cause for concern however; if the new idea or the system fails to work perfectly the first time, people may plunge back into chaos and seek to return to old status quo.

Implementation

Implementation involves putting the plan into place and making the changes for the first time. It's a period of excitement and challenge. It's a difficult stage and requires perseverance and buy-in from others. Support is a must to keep everyone on plan and to assure people of the value of the new vision (resulting in a new status quo). A solid action plan is a must and often has to be "sold" to those involved with or affected by the change.

Chaos and its negative emotions are still in place during implementation because the idea is not fully proven, and effectiveness may not have reached desired levels. There may still be significant resistance from those who fear change or who don't see what's in it for them. Effectiveness may fall even further until the full effect of the implementation can be felt. Therefore, old status quo or even chaos can still seem more comfortable than the new vision which individuals or the system have yet to experience.

Positive Emotions	Negative Emotions
• Excitement	• Fear
• Exhilaration	• Anxiety
• Confidence	• Uncertainty
• Satisfaction	• Pressure
• Comfort	• Confusion
• Security	• Resistance

Practice

This is the most undervalued but important stage in the process. There is a new vision of a new status quo, but ironically positive emotions, comfort, and satisfaction are the biggest dangers. These are the emotions that cause people to neglect this critical stage and ultimately fail to permanently change habits and behaviors. Until the new status quo becomes habit and is perfected, systems won't achieve full effectiveness and benefit. Training and practice are critical to making the new status quo a way of life and, therefore, a permanent change.

Remember, there is still chaos present as people try out new techniques or new ways of doing or looking at things. They can experience failure with their first attempts at new behaviors, and they still may feel more comfortable and capable with old status quo.

Practice or training can be boring or tedious (but it doesn't necessarily have to be). Many family businesses avoid practice and training for just this reason. Some people in the system want the solutions to be handed to them rather than having to work for them. The result too often is failure and reversion to chaos or old status quo.

Positive Emotions	Negative Emotions
• Excitement	• Fear
• Exhilaration	• Frustration
• Confidence	• Boredom

• Satisfaction	• Anxiety
• Comfort	• Pressure
• Security	• Confusion

During the implementation and practice stages, order is beginning to evolve, but it's important to support an environment where it's okay to ask questions and undertake new learning. The goal during integration and practice is to get control of the learning process and schedules, and to perfect the model in order to achieve a new, more productive status quo.

New Status Quo

In new status quo, the system and the family business are in a new place and are functioning at higher levels than before. New status quo is not reached as a permanent change until fully implemented and practiced and its usefulness fully realized. Keep in mind: new status quo quickly becomes the old comfort zone. Once the newness wears off, the rate of increase in effectiveness generally peaks and flattens. Thus, a new change is eventually needed to accelerate effectiveness once again; this is the essence of a continuous improvement process. The new status quo is just a stopping point to refuel until the next challenge or vision acts as a catalyst to thrust us back into the change process. After going through repeated changes, people and organizations learn how to learn, and new introductions of foreign elements or catalysts produce less anxiety, more excitement, and more opportunities for everyone to grow and prosper.

Conclusion

Change, instead of being a fearful and anxiety producing phenomenon, can be understood, explained rationally, and eventually mastered for the benefit of everyone in the family business system. Understanding the seven steps universal to any human system undergoing change is a great way to prepare yourself, your family, and

your business for the changes associated with transition or changes forced
upon you from outside foreign elements or catalysts

CHAPTER TEN

THE ULTIMATE GOAL:
HEALTHY FAMILIES AND HEALTHY BUSINESSES

PRESCRIPTION: Using highly successful business families as benchmarks, determine what it means to you to have a healthy family and a healthy business working together in harmony for mutual good. Work to reach the balance and proportion available in both.

Family business commentator Richard Beckhard estimates that the average life span of a family owned business is only 24 years. That length of time happens to coincide almost identically with the span of time that the average family business founder remains active in management. Why is perpetuating the family business so difficult? The answers are too numerous to count and can vary from business to business and family to family. As we have seen in previous chapters, conflicts abound in family business. Among them are:

- Disagreements over family issues.
- Disagreements over business issues.
- Conflicts over the boundaries between family and business.

Many of the conflicts arise because the family has not engaged in a process to define what their success should look like. We'll discuss below some benchmarks for healthy families and healthy businesses for you to use as you evaluate your own missions.

WHAT DO STRONG FAMILIES LOOK LIKE?

To answer the question above we must come up with two sets of definitions. First, what do healthy families look like? Second, what do healthy families *not* look like? The question must have two answers: the positive aspects of healthy family life and the negative aspects of unhealthy family life. Let's begin by looking at some of the positive traits of healthy families:

Commitment

Healthy families are committed to each other as individuals and to the family as a whole. The commitment is strong and unwavering. Healthy families know that there is no greater source of strength, support, nurturing, and love than the nuclear and extended family. Family is the source of origin and training and the launching pad for everything that we'll become in life as adults. The commitment to family should always be *first*.

Mutual Respect

Mutual respect is an essential element in healthy families. Even when members of the family don't agree with each other, the disagreements can be taken from positions of mutual respect. Ugliness and bitterness have no place in healthy family business life. It is okay to disagree with other members of the family, but it is not okay to behave in a disrespectful or disdainful manner toward other family members (this applies whether or not the disrespect takes place in a face-to-face setting).

Structured and Sacred Time Together

Families often behave in a backward fashion when it comes to family time together. Business appointments, doctor appointments, sporting events, etc. are considered to be sacred time commitments, and it is a sin to be late for any of these events. However, when it comes to family time, scheduling is a casual thing, and punctuality and even attendance are casually regarded.

Motivational speaker Zig Ziglar illustrates the point further; he says that during the workweek, we get up early, shower, put on our nicest clothes, and put forward our best appearances as we go out into the workplace. On weekends, however, we get up late, are sloppy about our hygiene, throw on old sweat pants, and generally behave like slobs. Why is it all right to put forward such a slothful and sloppy appearance for the people who we love the most and who mean the most in our lives? Shouldn't we behave in the opposite manner? If we are going to show slothfulness in our appearances, shouldn't it be casual acquaintances rather than members of our very own families who see us at less than our best? Ziglar's point may be slightly exaggerated, but he does provide an indication of how we do not consider our family time as sacred.

Clear Communication

Healthy families communicate directly and openly with each other. They avoid triangling where third parties do the dirty work. If one member of a healthy family has a problem with another, he simply approaches that person directly and discusses the matter in non-accusatory, safe language which expresses his point without accusation or acrimony.

Some families obviously have better communication skills than others. Some simply have never learned healthy communication or dispute resolution techniques. Once these fairly simple techniques are learned and absorbed, the family can take its communication to a higher level.

Strong, Shared Values

Most business families don't take the time to address directly who they are and what they want to be as families. Stephen Covey, in his book *The Seven Habits Of Highly Effective Families*, stresses that the most important exercise a family can engage in to define itself is the development of a Family Mission Statement. This exercise is a wonderful pursuit for a family in a retreat setting. It helps define the vision for what your healthy family should look like, what your family stands for, what the values of your family are, and how you would like to represent your family to the outside world.

Intimacy

Healthy families can express intimacy with each other without anxiety. Healthy families say they love each other; you would be surprised how many families have difficulty expressing this simple sentiment. It is important not only to say that you love other members of your family, it is also important to demonstrate it with your time, attention, respect, service, and support. Other ways to demonstrate intimacy with members of your family are to give nonverbal signals like touching. Active listening is also a great way to send the right message.

Trust

Healthy families trust each other to look out for them and to be dependable. One of the easiest ways to lose a person's trust is to be undependable. For example, if a family member is depending on you for baby-sitting, and you "forget" two or three times in a row, that erodes the level of trust. Members of your family have to trust that you will always come through for them.

Shared Power

Healthy families share power in the way they make decisions. Everyone's input is valuable and is considered as the family arrives at consensus decisions. Families run as dictatorships with decrees coming from above do not function effectively. In that way families are very different from family businesses where one strong leader often makes bold, sweeping, autocratic decisions for the good of the entrepreneurial company. Families are places where major questions must be presented openly, discussed thoroughly, and decided upon as a group where everyone's opinions can be heard and affirmed.

Independence

We earlier discussed the term enmeshment where families are too closely interconnected and boundaries are not established. Some families are smothering in the amount of attention they lavish on each other. Individuals are not allowed to become independent from the family as a whole; every decision, no matter how small, is a family decision. Healthy families allow for a strong measure of independence. Children who are born into family businesses may find that their childhoods are artificially extended, and they are not given enough space to truly discover themselves. Healthy families allow individual family members the room necessary to grow and prosper as individuals while still remaining true to the ideals of closeness and togetherness as a family.

CHARACTERISTICS OF AT RISK FAMILIES

Pervasive Family Tension

Excessive family tension stems from having a crisis attitude about every event in the life of the family regardless of how trivial. A call from a family member indicating that he is not feeling well immediately snowballs into the family assuming that a medical emergency looms, and the family must mobilize all its resources. It is important to have perspective in every aspect of your life, especially in family life. Negative attitudes and doom and gloom mentalities create worry, anxiety, and unnecessary tension in the life of the family.

Failure to Let Go and Forgive

Some families in business together seem to have an inability to let go of past slights or hurts. At every family meeting, the same story about how Dad behaved irresponsibly with the company's finances back in the 1980's comes up. "If only Dad hadn't made that terrible deal back in 1987, we would be sitting pretty today." Dad acted in a way that he thought best for the company, the family, and himself when he made that decision; there was no overt attempt to make a poor decision. He wasn't trying to harm anyone. Healthy families let bygones be bygones and forgive people for past mistakes. This does not mean that we are not accountable for our decisions, but that past misjudgments will not be allowed to resonate throughout the family for all time.

Pressure To Come Into the Family Business

Healthy families allow individuals to find their own way in

career choices. Unhealthy families force individuals to come back into the family business through any number of tactics. Requiring a young family member to select a career which is not her first, second, or even fifth choice is a surefire recipe for creating family and business problems. The choice to come to work in the family business should be arrived at freely, and family or financial pressure should not be the lever that thrusts a family member into employment against her wishes.

Pressure to Work As Hard As Dad (Or Granddad)

Some family business owners are absolutely ridiculous when it comes to their demands that all family members put in the same amount of hours they do. Entrepreneurial FBOs are obsessed with their companies and cheerfully work 16 hour days (or longer). These happen to be the same FBOs who wake up at age 60 or 65 and find their health ruined, their families resentful, and their prospects for a satisfying old age gone. One FBO was so obsessed about his business that he stopped coming home to sleep. He would simply take a two or three hour power nap on the couch in his office. He trained himself over time to get by on four hours of sleep per night. It wasn't unusual for his employees or advisors to get a call at 4:30 am. For this FBO, it was just part of the normal workday.

It is unreasonable to think that your children or grandchildren are going to have the same obsession with working that the founder did. Mature companies require a very different management style from startup, entrepreneurial companies. People work at different efficiencies; what takes one individual 10 hours to accomplish may take another individual only five. Today's adults seek more balance in their lives among work, family, and leisure. They're not inclined to want to work every weekend or spend 16 hours a day at the office to the detriment of their young children. It is imperative that senior members of family businesses recognize that their children have different needs and work habits and accept these work habits. A ridiculous demand of a mandatory 12 or 16 hour work day is a sure way to alienate junior generation family employees *and* their spouses.

Inability To Let Family Members Learn From Their Own Mistakes

We all want our children and grandchildren to benefit from our experiences and avoid some of the painful mistakes we made as we grew up - this is a normal human sentiment. However, we must give our children and grandchildren the freedom to make their own mistakes and learn from the school of hard knocks as we did. We can't shelter them in every aspect of their lives and expect them to be confident, capable decision-makers as they mature. Healthy family members resist the urge to meddle in the affairs of other family members and advise them on every aspect of human existence. If you have done a good job of providing unconditional love and support to members of your own family, chances are they will have the wisdom and foresight to come to you when your advice is necessary. If you have been smothering with your advice and have meddled in every aspect of your child's life, that is going to have the perverse effect of causing the child to avoid you at the very times when your advice is the most necessary. Giving advice, like so many other things in life, should be done in moderation. We must give our children and grandchildren enough room to make mistakes and learn from them.

Gossiping

Some families are veritable soap operas when it comes to gossip-ing about each other. Gossip is destructive in society at large, but can be exponentially destructive in families. Some family members can't seem to wait to pick up the phone and call the brother-in-law to report what he just heard from Dad. The brother-in-law passes the information along (distorted of course). It gets passed along again, and again, until the entire family is in an uproar over an item that should never have been communicated in the first place. Healthy families communicate directly and clearly; gossip has no place.

Avoidance Of Family Functions

Some family members will go to great lengths to avoid getting together with the rest of the family. Healthy families spend quality, sacred, structured time together regularly. It shows disrespect and disdain for the sanctity of the family when a few family members regularly fail to show up for designated family functions. Another way they can undermine the validity of the function is to arrive very late or leave very early - their participation in the family event is perfunctory and conditional. Healthy families interact together and have fun together. Family gatherings may not be as fun as going to ball games or heading for the beach, but they are a necessary - even vital part - of healthy family life and should be respected as such.

WHAT DO HEALTHY FAMILY COMPANIES LOOK LIKE?

Like the healthy family traits discussed above, healthy family company traits are two-sided coins too. We must examine both the positive aspects of companies as well as the negative aspects of unhealthy companies. The following are positive traits of healthy family business:

Family's Support Of The Company Is Strong

Healthy family businesses are characterized by the support and pride of the family which began or owns the enterprise. Whether or not a family member is an employee, he should give his unconditional support to the family enterprise in public. One of the most destructive things a family member can do is to go around town carping and backbiting over every decision the family business makes. Telling everyone in town that you disagree with the decisions the company leaders make is a bitter and demeaning exercise for all involved. Comments like "I can't believe they are spending all that money to remodel the building. It is a terrible waste of resources. I can't believe how lavish that facility is. They just think they are so much better than the rest of us" are the kinds of comments that community gossips love to hear. Rest assured that bitter, negative comments like the ones above get into the community grapevine faster than the speed of sound and will ultimately cause disharmony between employee and non-employee members of the family business.

The Business Is Financially Sound

Family companies that are continually struggling for mere survival are not attractive places to work for members of founding or subsequent generations. The daily pressure to remain afloat doesn't allow for the flowering of individuals' real capabilities. Consultant Paul Coffman has identified the three reasons for the failure of every business plan:

1. The objectives were not realistic.
2. The plan was not adequate.
3. The people did not execute the plan.

In a business that is struggling for survival, each of the three components of the business plan listed above must be examined carefully.

The financially sound family business, on the other hand, is a place that attracts family and non-family employees like a magnet. It is a place where there are sufficient opportunities for personal and professional growth and advancement. It is a place where people are fairly and equitably compensated for the work they produce and one that encourages them to take on additional training and education in an effort to grow. The successful family business is a source of tremendous family pride, and there is enthusiasm for the continued growth and pro-ductivity of the business that has laid golden eggs for the business family.

The Business Is Organizationally Sound

Since most family businesses are started by "technicians suffering from entrepreneurial seizures," they are not initially heavy on structure and organization. However, as a family business matures and the second or perhaps even the third generation is ready to come aboard, the company must have structure and organization if it is to be effective in the future. Operating by the seat of the pants with the founder keeping all critical information in his head is no longer adequate.

Healthy family businesses have real, live, functioning organizational charts. They have written business plans that look five to 10 years into the future. They have written marketing plans with details that spell out how they are going to secure future business and what it should mean for the company. They have written succession plans for how family members can enter the company, what it takes to enter management, what it takes to gain ownership, and determines who will lead the company.

Abraham Lincoln once said that if he had eight hours to chop a cord of wood, he would spend the first four hours sharpening his ax. Healthy family businesses take the time to sharpen their axes and create functioning organizations.

Successor Generations Have Outside Business Experience

Healthy family businesses encourage the children of successor generations to gather experience at places outside their family companies. There are several reasons why this is a healthy family business trait. First, it avoids some of the stigma of having family employees come in as members of the "lucky sperm club." If a family member was employed at another organization, did well, enjoyed success, and subsequently came back into the family firm, he is much more likely to have at least the grudging approval of the employees. Second, if a family member has work experience in another organization, he will have new skills and perspectives to bring home to the family business that could enrich the enterprise. Third, working at a place other than the family business will give the young person a chance to build his confidence. He will have demonstrated that he can succeed independent of his family and his family's business. This can be a great boost to his self-esteem and provide a great launching pad for success in the family company.

Does this mean that a family member who has never worked outside the family company is doomed to failure? Not at all. It simply means that in most instances, it is very desirable, practically and psychologically, for family members to work outside their families of origin for a time.

Willingness to Let Trusted Employees, Advisors, Or Outsiders Challenge the Old Status Quo

Healthy family businesses are confident in their decision-making abilities. They are not afraid of challenging the status quo or interjecting the possibility of a new way of doing things. They're intellectually curious and are always willing to look at new perspectives and new procedures which might enhance the operation of the family company. Healthy family businesses retain the ultimate power for decision-making in the hands of one or a small group of officers; however, they welcome the input of others in the organization from rank and file employees to upper management. Everyone works for the common goal of making the company more profitable and more effective in its operations.

Change Is Embraced As Healthy, Necessary, And Inevitable

Healthy family companies don't fear the future. They have met and conquered challenges and know they can do so again as the future unfolds. The individuals who operate successful family companies are willing to learn and grow as people and professionals. Everyone is unsettled by the prospect of change to one degree or another, but truly successful family companies embrace change, see the opportunities associated with it, and seek continual improvement.

Common Vision

Successful family companies have a common vision of what their businesses will look like when they're mature. Much like healthy families that work together to build a consensus family mission statement, healthy family companies work together to build consensus for a business vision statement. Most companies today have a framed mission statement created by an individual or a committee. The statement is typed up, framed, hung on the wall, and forgotten. A business vision is more compelling. The business vision is the measuring stick against which all decisions are compared. Decisions are either "on-purpose" or "off-purpose" when it comes to fulfilling the vision. Just as the family mission statement is most critical for assuring the continuation of a successful family, the business vision statement is the most critical exercise for developing a common, comprehensive picture for what the family enterprise should ultimately become.

FAMILY BUSINESS BEHAVIORS TO AVOID

TTWWADIH

"That's the way we've always done it here." Those eight words spell out a death sentence. These businesses fear change, fail to adapt, remain mired in yesterday's way of doing business, and cannot possibly hope to succeed as change unfolds at a faster and faster pace. These are the companies that refuse to modernize, professionalize, organize, and strategize. They are not open to challenge from insiders or outsiders. Simply put, they have created a Great Wall of China around their businesses and their people, and they will be satisfied as long as they can protect the status quo.

No Systems in Place

These companies are still run as entrepreneurial companies

where the founder makes all decisions based on gut instinct. He is intensely private and keeps all the important business facts in his head with communication to other members of the business family on a need-to-know basis only. If this type of family business leader is struck down by illness or death, his successor managers are left to sink or swim depending on their abilities. This is a recipe for family business disaster.

Poor Financial Performance

Motivational speaker Brian Tracey quotes a Dun and Bradstreet study which distilled the one true secret of business success. He says that companies fail because of "low sales." Other companies succeed because of "high sales." What could be simpler than that? Family businesses that fail find themselves in declining markets with flat or falling sales, yet try to employ the same old business tactics in the face of failure. They are afflicted with the Alcoholics Anonymous definition of insanity: they do the same thing over and over hoping to get different results. Healthy companies are proactive and look inside and outside their organizations for help that can vault them to the next level. They don't wait for a period of stagnation and decline to make repairs. Their motto is "if it ain't broke, fix it anyway."

Family Members Look At the Family Company As a "Free Ride"

Some family companies have a nepotism policy that is stated simply as "if your last name is Jones, you are guaranteed a management job and ownership in the family company." Family members come to look at this type of organization as an entitlement. Whether or not they have a burning desire to succeed, they know they can come into the family business, make a comfortable living, enjoy status as members of a leading business family in the community, and go on cruise control for the rest of their adult lives. This may work in some family firms for a time, but it is ultimately a recipe for disaster. Successful family firms have clear rules about who can enter the company, who can manage the company, and who can own stock in it.

The Senior Generation Won't Let Go

A mid-sixties family business owner hired consultants to advise him on how to ease out of his company while moving his children into management. For six days he worked with consultants doing analysis, design, and implementation of selected strategies. On the last day of the engagement his son reported that he had authorized a superintendent to purchase a $1,500 laptop computer. Dad hit the ceiling. He thought it was an unnecessary, extravagant waste of money, and he told his son in no uncertain terms in front of other employees. The son, who was very encouraged by the hiring of consultants to help ease the transition, was devastated. He could see the handwriting on the wall; this dad was never going to be able to let go.

Senior generation family members must force themselves to step back from the enterprises they have created and nurtured. To fail to do so can do irreparable harm to the business and the family. This doesn't mean that founders or senior generation family members can't have productive, even lucrative, roles in their family enterprises. It just means that they have to let someone else make most of the decisions. They must force themselves to become consultants and teachers rather than managers and doers.

The four lists above will help you recognize both positive and negative family and business traits and benchmark yourself and your family company against them. As an additional self-test, see the survey "Eighty Questions Every Family Business Owner Should Answer" in the Appendix.

Conclusion

Family businesses are changing faster now than ever before. In the "old" family business model;

- The founder worked and retained power in the enterprise until his death.
- After his demise, the firm was passed on to the oldest son.
- Daughters were generally not allowed in the family business, or they worked in support or clerical roles.
- The entrepreneur kept all information between his ears and shared with other family members - even his wife - strictly on a need-to-know basis.
- Change was not as rapid, and the need for evolutionary thinking was not as critical.

The modern family business looks different:

- The founder works to transfer management and ownership during his lifetime.
- He seeks an exit strategy from the business that will give him fulfillment, financial security, and satisfaction in his golden years.
- The firm can be passed along to anyone regardless of sex or whether or not they are family members. A valued non-family manager can ultimately inherit or buy the family company.
- There is a greater degree of separation between family and business. There is recognition that the responsibilities and demands of each are different.
- Women are in positions of authority and decision-making. They are no longer relegated to support or clerical roles.
- Family and business issues are discussed openly in the appropriate settings. Secrecy and silence are no longer hallmarks of family business management.

The family business has come a long way in the last generation. The accelerating pace of change in the family enterprise is likely to continue.   Healthy families and healthy businesses embrace change as inevitable and seek to plan for change in such a way that perpetuates the wonderful attributes that make them unique and discards the harmful characteristics that hold them back.

APPENDIX

The 10 Prescriptions for a Healthy Family Business

1. Create awareness of yourself, your family, and your business. Address the four dynamics of the family enterprise as a whole rather than as individual, unrelated parts.

2. Recognize that successful family business owners are pursuing the two dreams that all heroes (from ancient mythology to the present) pursue - the dreams of heroic mission and heroic stature. Ultimately, both are illusory.

3. Recognize and understand that there are evolutionary forces beyond your control that are partially driving the way you think and feel. Learn how those forces affect your business and family lives.

4. Since FAMILY is the critical part of the family business enterprise; be aware of the nature of changing families and develop decision-making systems to support both the family and the business.

5. Avoid the 10 most common estate and succession planning errors of family business owners. Any one of them could devastate your company, tear apart your family, or BOTH!

6. Your business family must develop an organized, formal, and regularly scheduled mechanism for improving and sustaining sound communications.

7. Because your departure from your business is inevitable, plan and write out a specific program for your exit and the ascension of the next generation of leaders in your business.

8. Provide for the distribution of the wealth you have created in a way that does not retard or undermine your children's opportunities to

become valuable, productive members of society.

9. Understanding that change is inevitable, transform yourself and your organization from focusing on maintaining the status quo to learning, continually growing, and seeking new opportunities for improvement.

10. Using highly successful business families as benchmarks, determine what it means to you to have a healthy family and a healthy business working together in harmony for mutual good. Work to reach the balance and proportion available in both.

80 Questions Every Family Business Owner Should Answer

Family Relationships

1. Are the family members employed by the business compensated fairly and adequately? Upon what standard is their compensation based?

2. Rate the quality of communication within your business family on a 1 to 10 scale with 10 being perfect. If your response is "6" or less, what are the contributing factors?

3. If you were to poll the other family members in your business and your key employees, is there an explicitly agreed upon vision for where your family company is headed in the next 5 years? If not, why not?

4. Are there regularly scheduled meetings for the purpose of working ON the family, communication, and relationships?

5. Is there a proven methodology that you employ for resolving conflict in your family?

6. When there are difficult decisions to be made, is there a proven methodology for arriving at decisions or do you often decide "not to decide" in order to preserve harmony?

7. Are there rules for entry of family members into business management?

8. Are there rules for entry of family members into business ownership?

9. Is the future ownership of your family company clearly defined? If not, why not?

10. Is there the potential for ownership in your family enterprise to be fragmented in the future (or right now) so no one person controls? If so, what anti-deadlock provisions have you got in place?

11. At this stage in your business life, being brutally honest, is your business generally adding to the quality of your life, or is it gradually draining the energy and quality of life away from you?

12. What, ultimately, do you want to get out of the business? Why do you work as hard as you do?

13. What is one item in your family or business that has been nagging you for some time and that you've been meaning to clean up? What is holding you back from cleaning up this persistent, uncomfortable issue?

14. What's the one relationship in your family or business family that causes you the most concern? If that relationship were to improve dramatically, what types of benefits would you see?

15. What objective criteria do you use in evaluating your children's strengths, weaknesses, skills, and talents as you attempt to evaluate their potential as successors? Where are you most confident in them? Doubtful?

Exit Planning

16. If you own a business with siblings or cousins of the same generation, what are your exit plans? Are you inadvertently creating a race for the door between same generation owners where the first one to get out wins?

17. What are your provisions for you to exit your business with financial security assured?

18. Is there a liquidity plan for buying back the stock of departing shareholders?

19. How many hours per week are you working now? Are you working harder or less hard than you did 5 years ago? If you're working harder now, what is your plan for gradually slowing down and enjoying some of the fruits of your labor?

20. How much time do you take away from the business for rest and relaxation (vacations at your industry or trade conventions or when you do work at home or at the beach don't count)? Ideally, how much time would you like to take off? What's holding you back from having as much vacation time as you would like?

21. On a 1 to 10 scale with 10 being perfect, how well do you think you manage your time? If your answer is a "6" or below, what do you have to do to get your time management and personal effectiveness skills up to an acceptable level?

"Drop Dead" Planning

22. Have your wills and associated trust documents been updated in the past 3 years? If not, why not?

23. Do you have the following: Declaration for Desire of Natural Death, Power of Attorney, and Healthcare Power of Attorney? If not, why not?

24. Do your testamentary documents assure your family business privacy after your death?

25. Are your assets titled properly between you and your spouse in order to take maximum advantage of the estate tax laws?

26. Do your testamentary documents specifically address the disposition of your family business?

27. Do your testamentary documents agree with other business arrangements such as buy-sell agreements?

28. Do you pass ownership of the family company to your spouse in your testamentary documents as a tax avoidance measure? If so, does that make practical sense, and is that consistent with the wishes of your spouse?

29. If the business ownership does go to your spouse, is there the potential for your children to inflate his/her estate thereby increasing their estate tax burden during his/her surviving lifetime?

30. What are your testamentary provisions for treating your employee and non-employee children fairly and equitably?

31. In your "drop dead" planning, do you have insurance proceeds includable in your taxable estate? If so, why?

32. For your real estate, do you use Family Limited Partnerships or Limited Liability Companies? If not, why not?

33. If there is more than one shareholder in your family enterprise, do you have a binding, modern buy-sell agreement? If not, why not?

34. Does your agreement cover atypical items such as disability, "bad boy" behavior, windfall sale, non-compete provisions, etc.?

35. Do you have a written plan for when your family members get

home from your funeral to lessen the burden on them? If not, why not?

36. In the future, will your business go to family members, some of whom are employed in the company and some of whom are not? If so, what provisions will you make to balance the interests of employee shareholders versus non-employee shareholders?

37. If you were to drop dead, could your family and/or business survive the "triple whammy" of loss of the family patriarch, loss of a key family business manager, and the potential for ruinous estate taxation? What is your contingency plan?

38. Your CPA, attorney, and other advisors have probably been after you for some time to address the issues of your exit, future management of the company, your estate planning, etc. What are the barriers that prevent you from tackling these tough family business issues?

39. Do you worry about giving your children too much in the way of assets too soon? What do you see as the downside of "affluenza"?

40. Will your children inherit the business in equal portions or will one child be designated the "prize pig" and receive a larger proportion? What are the pros and cons of each course of action?

General Closely Held Business Questions

41. List your top 5 frustrations in the family business.

42. Thinking objectively, what are the marketing strengths of your family business?

43. Thinking objectively, what are the sales strengths of your family business?

44. Thinking objectively, what are the operational strengths of your family business?

45. Thinking objectively, what are the administrative strengths of your family business?

46. Thinking objectively, what are the marketing weaknesses in your family business?

47. Thinking objectively, what are the sales weaknesses in your family business?

48. Thinking objectively, what are the operational weaknesses in your family business?

49. Thinking objectively, what are the administrative weaknesses in your family business?

50. What do you consider to be the main threats facing your business in the next three years?

51. If your family business were to fail in the next three years, what would you predict would be the most likely cause(s)?

52. Being brutally honest, can you recite your company's mission statement by memory? If not, why not?

53. Are there regularly scheduled meetings for the purpose of working *ON* the business?

54. Is there a proven methodology that you employ for resolving conflict in your business?

55. What skills or training do you need to be more successful in the family enterprise?

56. What skills or training do other people need to be more successful in the family enterprise?

57. How profitable are you versus your peers in your industry? Into what percentile do you fall? What are the reasons for your position?

58. What are your corporate goals for this year? If you were to assess other managers in your company, would their goals be the same? Are you all on the same page?

59. Is the future management of your family company clearly defined? If not, why not?

60. Do you use a formal or informal Board of Advisors or Board of Directors? If not, why not?

61 Do you have regular senior management meetings to discuss your strategic plan, business plan, capital plan, human resources, etc? If not, why not?

62. Do you have a written organization chart for your enterprise and do you manage to the organization chart, or is it just a nice piece of wallpaper?

63. Do you have the right people (especially family members) in the right positions in the company for now (and for the future)?

64. Do you have written job descriptions for family and non-family employees? If not, why not?

65. Is the authority embodied in the job descriptions defined and supported? If not, why not?

66. Do you regularly conduct employee performance reviews and schedule sessions for appropriate feedback? If not, why not?

67. Being as objective as you can, if you were to evaluate your top 10 family business employees and the jobs they are doing, if you were to start your business from scratch tomorrow, would you hire them again? If not, why not?

68. Do you have a customer satisfaction program in place that gives you formal feedback about how your customers view your company? If not, why not?

69. Do you know what your "critical success factors" are for your business? If not, why not?

70. From a sales standpoint, what are your competitive advantages? Disadvantages?

71. Who is the next leader of the family enterprise? Is this clear to everyone, or a big secret and potentially a bone of contention?

72. Are there rules for distributions of funds from your family enterprise (above and beyond employment compensation)?

73. Are there policies in place for appropriate handling of corporate profits in order to balance the needs of the corporation, employee shareholders, and non-employee shareholders?

74. If you didn't come to work for the next 6 months for whatever reason, in what condition would your business be upon your return? What would likely have happened to your most valuable asset during your absence? Why?

75. At this stage in the evolution of the family company, what is your return on investment (both financial and non-financial)? Are you getting a sufficient rate of return to fairly compensate for your blood, toil, sweat, and tears?

76. What new capabilities must you, your employees, or your company acquire to stay competitive over the next 5 years?

77. If you don't have children who are capable of taking over the business at your retirement, what is the best course of action? Should you close the doors, sell it to insiders, or sell it to outsiders?

78. You've made a decision to hire some new talent; how do you objectively quantify the candidates' qualifications for the job and abilities to do the job effectively?

79. What are your recruiting processes when it's time to hire new talent? Do you have formal procedures that can produce predictable results, or is it an informal process that more closely resembles a crapshoot?

80. What are the three most important things you should focus on in your job that would be the most productive for your company in the next 90 days? Once you've identified those three items, determine approximately how much time, as a percentage, you're currently spending on those critical success items. If you spent more time on those key items, what kind of results could you produce for yourself and the company?

5 BONUS QUESTIONS:

1. What do you have **TOO MUCH** of in your business?

2. What do you have **TOO LITTLE** of in your business?

3. What do you have **TOO MUCH** of in your family?

4. What do you have **TOO LITTLE** of in your family?

5. If you had a magic wand, what would be the one thing you would change about your family or business?

BIBLIOGRAPHY

Bork, David
Family Business, Risky Business: How to Make It Work
Bork Institute for Family Business, 1993

Bork, David; Jaffe, Dennis T.; Lane, Sam H.; Dashew, Leslie; Heisler, Quentin G.
Working with Family Businesses: A Guide for Professionals
Jossey-Bass Publishers, 1996

Covey, Stephen R.
First Things First
Fireside, 1994

Frankenberg, Ellen, PhD
Your Family, Inc.: Practical Tips for Building a Healthy Family Business
The Haworth Mental Health Press, 1999

Gerber, Michael E.
The E-Myth Revisited
HarperCollins Publishers, 1995

Gersick, Kelin E.; Davis, John A.; Hampton, Marion McCollom; Lansberg, Ivan
Generation to Generation: Life Cycles of the Family Business
Harvard Business School Press, 1997

Hoover, Edwin A. and Hoover, Colette Lombard
Getting Along in Family Business: The Relationship Intelligence Handbook
Routledge, 1999

Jaffe, Dennis T., PhD
Working With the Ones You Love: Strategies for a Successful Family Business
Conari Press, 1991

Jones, Laurie Beth
The Path: Creating Your Mission Statement For Work And For Life
Hyperion, 1996

Keirsey, David
Please Understand Me II
Prometheus Nemesis Book Company, 1998

Lansberg, Ivan
Succeeding Generations: Realizing the Dream of Families in Business
Harvard Business School Press, 1999

Lea, James W., PhD
Keeping It in the Family: Successful Succession of The Family Business
John Wiley & Sons, Inc., 1991

Levinson, Daniel J.
The Seasons Of A Man's Life
Ballantine Books, 1978

Satir, Virginia
The New PeopleMaking
Science and Behavior Books, Inc., 1988

Sheehy, Gail
Understanding Men's Passages
Random House, 1998

Sonnenfeld, Jeffrey
The Hero's Farewell: What Happens When CEOs Retire
Harvard Business School, 1988

Stanley, Thomas J., PhD; Danko, William D., PhD
The Millionaire Next Door
Longstreet Press, 1996

Stursberg, Peter A.
One-Day Business Planning and Everyday Follow-Up
Chilton Company, 1988

For more information on the services and products of
The Family Business Institute, Inc.
please visit our website at
www.familybusinessinstitute.com